STUDY GUIDE WITH COMPUTER APPLICATIONS

David W. Oakes
University of Illinois

STRATEGIC COMPENSATION
Second Edition

Joseph J. Martocchio

Upper Saddle River, New Jersey 07458

Acquisitions editor: Melissa Steffens
Assistant editor: Jessica Sabloff
Production editor: Carol Zaino
Manufacturer: Victor Graphics

Copyright ©2001 by Prentice-Hall, Inc., Upper Saddle River, New Jersey, 07458. All rights reserved. Printed in the United States of America. This publication is protected by copyright, and permission should be obtained from the publisher prior to any prohibited reproduction, storage in a retrieval system, or transmission in any form or by any means, electronic, mechanical, photocopying, recording, or likewise. For information regarding permission(s), write to: Rights and Permissions Department.

ISBN 0-13-029070X

10 9 8 7 6 5 4 3 2 1

CONTENTS

Preface

Suggested Study Approach

Chapter 1	COMPENSATION: A COMPONENT OF HUMAN RESOURCE SYSTEMS	1
Chapter 2	STRATEGIC COMPENSATION IN ACTION: STRATEGIC ANALYSIS AND CONTEXTUAL FACTORS	13
Chapter 3	CONTEXTUAL INFLUENCES ON COMPENSATION PRACTICE	27
Chapter 4	TRADITIONAL BASES FOR PAY: SENIORITY AND MERIT	37
Chapter 5	INCENTIVE PAY	49
Chapter 6	PERSON-FOCUSED PAY	59
Chapter 7	BUILDING INTERNALLY CONSISTENT COMPENSATION SYSTEMS	69
Chapter 8	BUILDING MARKET-COMPETITIVE COMPENSATION SYSTEMS	83
Chapter 9	BUILDING PAY STRUCTURES THAT RECOGNIZE INDIVIDUAL CONTRIBUTIONS	93
Chapter 10	LEGALLY REQUIRED BENEFITS	105
Chapter 11	DISCRETIONARY BENEFITS	113
Chapter 12	INTERNATIONAL COMPENSATION	125
Chapter 13	COMPENSATING EXECUTIVES	135
Chapter 14	COMPENSATING THE FLEXIBLE WORK FORCE: CONTINGENT EMPLOYEES AND FLEXIBLE WORK SCHEDULES	145

Answers for the Fill-In the Blanks and
Multiple Choice Questions ... 155

STUDY GUIDE WITH COMPUTER APPLICATIONS

David W. Oakes
Brian M. Pianfetti
Mona L. Shannon

University of Illinois

Strategic Compensation:

A Human Resource Management Approach

Second Edition

Joseph J. Martocchio

PREFACE

This Study Guide with Computer Applications has been prepared to accompany *Strategic Compensation: A Human Resource Management Approach*, second edition, by Joseph J. Martocchio. The purpose of the study guide component is to promote your understanding of the text material and assist in your preparation for tests.

Each chapter contains the learning objectives, an outline of the material in the textbook, and key terms with page numbers that cross-reference the material in the textbook. Also, two sections of questions are included to help increase your understanding of the material. Questions include fill-in the blanks and multiple choice. Last, but certainly not least, each chapter concludes with the computer applications (exercises).

The computer exercises ask you to assume the role of Compensation Specialist for a fictitious company called Pizza Joe's. Pizza Joe's produces and sells frozen pizza products, including pizza snacks, full size pizzas, and personal sized pizzas. Sales are expanding as a result of a new patented process they have developed which keeps pizza crusts crispy in the microwave! The college crowd loves it.

Currently, Pizza Joe's has 2,000 employees, annual sales of 200 million dollars, and annual profits of 10 million dollars. They have adopted a differentiation strategy and expect sales and profits to continue to grow for at least the next three years. Strategic management of compensation and benefits will be important to their success. As a Compensation Specialist, you will be given 14 different assignments (exercises) designed to use compensation to help Pizza Joe's obtain a competitive advantage.

Each exercise in this supplement describes a situation at Pizza Joe's and asks you to answer specific questions. The accompanying software summarizes some of the information from the exercise and the questions. But, you must thoroughly review all the information contained in the corresponding description in this supplement before answering the questions on line.

The software allows you to record your answers on charts and/or answer sheets. Some questions will require that you identify and enter the appropriate information in a chart and the computer calculates the answer. Other questions direct you to use a calculator available on the software and enter the answer on a chart or answer sheet. After completing the exercise, click on the printer icon to print all of the questions and your answers.

The topics for the 14 exercises are:

        Exercise 1.   Costing Pay Increases

        Exercise 2.   Compensation System Review

Exercise 3.	Responding to Alleged Pay Discrimination
Exercise 4.	Comparing the Costs of Merit Pay vs. Merit Bonuses
Exercise 5.	Determining Current Profit Sharing Payouts
Exercise 6.	Implementing a Pay-for-knowledge Program
Exercise 7.	Conducting a Job Evaluation
Exercise 8.	Working with a Salary Survey
Exercise 9.	Evaluating a Merit Pay Structure
Exercise 10.	Estimating Unemployment Benefits
Exercise 11.	Costing Discretionary Benefits
Exercise 12.	International Compensation: Preparing a Balance Sheet
Exercise 13.	Analyzing Executive Compensation
Exercise 14.	Compensating Temporary Employees

A CD-ROM for IBM-compatible computers contain the software to accompany the exercises in this supplement. Installation is easy. After putting the CD-ROM in the appropriate drive, *Windows 95* (and more recent versions) users should click the Start button and select Run. Then, type a:\setup. *Windows 3.x* users should click on the File menu and select Run. Then, type a:\setup. In either case, you will be prompted through the installation process. After installing the program, please select the brief guided tour which will familiarize you with the features of the program.

A version of this software for Macintosh users may be downloaded from the *Strategic Compensation* web site (http://www.prenhall.com/martocchio).

SUGGESTED STUDY APPROACH

Students should read the textbook material first. As you read through the chapters, give thought to the learning objectives at the beginning of each chapter, and the key terms listed at the end of each chapter. In addition, keep in mind that the headings of each chapter correspond to the learning objectives. Studying the sections of the chapter in conjunction with the learning objectives should promote your understanding of the material and retention of the key concepts.

After reading each chapter in the textbook, you should review the corresponding material in the Study Guide. Start off by reviewing the learning objectives followed by the chapter outline. As you review these, think back to the main concepts and issues that you read about in the textbook. Then, move on to the key terms section. Review these, also giving thought to the material you read in the textbook. Finally, test your knowledge and understanding of the material by completing the Fill-In the Blank and Multiple Choice questions. Try not to look back at the key terms, chapter outline, or textbook material while you work on these. The answers to these questions are located at the end of this supplement. Review the material in the textbook for questions you have answered incorrectly and ask your course instructor to clarify questions you may have.

I welcome your comments and questions about *Strategic Compensation*, the study guide, or computer applications. Feel free to contact me by letter at the address below, by phone (217-244-4098), or by e-mail (martocch@uiuc.edu).

Best of luck!

Joe Martocchio
Institute of Labor and Industrial Relations
University of Illinois
504 East Armory Avenue
Champaign, IL 61820-6297

CHAPTER 1

Strategic Compensation: A Component of Human Resource Systems

Learning Objectives

1. Basic compensation concepts and the context of compensation practice
2. A historical perspective on compensation: From an administrative function to a strategic function
3. The difference between strategic and tactical compensation
4. Compensation professionals' goals within a human resources department
5. How compensation professionals relate to various stakeholders

Chapter Outline

I. **Exploring and Defining the Compensation Context**
   A. What Is Compensation?
      1. Core Compensation
      2. "Fringe" Compensation (Employee Benefits)

II. **A Historical Perspective on Compensation**
   A. The Road toward Strategic Compensation

III. **Strategic versus Tactical Compensation**
   A. Competitive Strategy Choices
   B. Tactical Decisions That Support the Firm's Strategy

IV. **Compensation Professionals' Goals within a Human Resource Department**
   A. How Human Resource Professionals Fit into the Corporate Hierarchy
   B. How the Compensation Function Fits into HR Departments
   C. The Compensation Department's Main Goals

V. **Stakeholders of the Compensation System**

Key Terms

Base pay represents the monetary compensation employees earn on a regular basis for performing their jobs. Hourly pay and salary are the main forms of base pay. (p. 4)

Compensable factors are job attributes (i.e., skill, effort, responsibility, and working conditions) that compensation professionals use to determine the value of jobs. (p. 4)

Compensation represents both the intrinsic and extrinsic rewards that employees receive for working. (p. 2)

Compensation surveys are used to determine how similar companies' compensation their employees. (p. 18)

Competitive advantage refers to a company's ability to maintain market share and profitability. (p.8)

Competitive strategy refers to the planned use of company resources to promote and sustain competitive advantage. (p. 9)

Core compensation refers to the monetary rewards given to employees for their job performance. (p. 4)

Cost leadership or (lowest cost) strategies focus on gaining competitive advantage by being the lowest cost producer. (p. 10)

Cost-of-living adjustments (COLAs) represent periodic base pay increases that are based on changes in prices, as indexed by the consumer price index (CPI). COLAs enable workers to maintain their purchasing power and standards of living by adjusting base pay for inflation. (p. 5)

Differentiation is a strategy used to develop products or services that are unique from those of its competitors. (p. 12)

Discretionary benefits are benefits that employers offer at their own choice. These benefits fall into three broad categories—protection programs, pay for time-not-worked, and services. (p. 7)

Early retirement programs contain incentives designed to encourage highly paid employees with substantial seniority to retire earlier than planned. (p. 16)

Employee benefits (fringe compensation) include any variety of programs that provide for pay for time-not-worked (i.e., vacation), employee services (i.e., transportation services), and protection programs (i.e., life insurance). (p. 6)

Extrinsic compensation includes both monetary and nonmonetary rewards. (p. 2)

Hourly pay or (wage) is one type of base pay. Employees earn hourly pay for each hour worked. (p. 4)

Human capital refers to an employees' knowledge and skills that enables them to be productive (see human capital theory). (p. 5)

Human capital theory states that employees' knowledge and skills generate productive capital known as human capital. Employees can develop knowledge and skills from formal education or on-the-job experiences. (p. 5)

Human resource strategies specify the particular use of HR practices to be consistent with competitive strategy. (p. 10)

Incentive pay (variable pay) rewards employees for partially or completely attaining a predetermined work objective. (p. 5)

Internally consistent compensation systems clearly define the relative value of each job among all jobs within a company. (p. 17)

Intrinsic compensation reflects employees' psychological mind-sets that result from performing their jobs. (p. 2)

Job analysis is a systematic process for gathering, documenting, and analyzing information in order to describe jobs. (p. 18)

Job evaluation reflects the values and priorities that management places on various positions. (p. 18)

Jobs characteristics theory describes the critical psychological states that employees experience when they perform their jobs (that is, intrinsic compensation). According to the job characteristics theory, employees experience enhanced psychological states when their jobs rate high on five core job dimensions—skill variety, task identity, task significance, autonomy, and feedback. (p. 3)

Legally required benefits are protection programs that attempt to promote worker safety and health, maintain family income streams, and assist families in crisis. The key legally-required benefits are mandated by the following laws—the Social Security Act of 1935, various state workers' compensation laws (see below), and the Family and Medical Leave Act of 1993. (p. 6)

Line employees are directly involved in producing companies' goods or in service delivery. Assembler, production worker, and sales employees are examples of line jobs. (p. 14)

Market-competitive pay systems represent companies' compensation policies that fit with companies' business objectives. (p. 18)

Merit pay programs base compensation on job performance. (p. 5)

Pay-for-knowledge a compensation plan that rewards managerial, service, and professional employees for successfully learning new business-related curricula. (p. 5)

Pay for time-not-worked represents discretionary employee benefits that provide employees time off with pay, such as vacation. (p. 7)

Pay grades group jobs for pay policy application and are based on similar compensable factors and values. (p. 18)

Pay ranges are the minimum, middle, and maximum amount of pay that each position is determined to be worth. (p. 18)

Pay structures represent pay rate differences for jobs of unequal worth and the framework for recognizing differences in employee contributions. (p. 18)

Pension programs provide income to individuals throughout their retirement. Sometimes, companies use early retirement programs to reduce workforce size and trim compensation expenditures. (p. 16)

Protection programs provide family benefits, promote health, and guard against income loss caused by catastrophic factors like unemployment, disability, or serious illness. (p. 7)

Salary is one type of base pay. Employees earn salaries for performing their jobs, regardless of the actual number of hours worked. Companies generally measure salary on an annual basis (p. 4)

Scientific management is a business practice that controls labor costs by replacing inefficient production methods with new ones. (p. 9)

Seniority pay rewards employees by increasing base pay based on the employee's length of service with the company. (p. 5)

Services represent discretionary employee benefits that provide enhancements to employees and their families like tuition reimbursement and day care assistance. (p. 7)

Severance pay is given to employees who are involuntarily laid off and generally includes several months pay and continued medical insurance coverage. (p. 16)

Skill-based pay is used mostly for employees who do physical work and increases their pay as they master new skills. (p. 5)

Staff employees support the functions performed by line employees. Human resources and accounting are examples of staff functions. (p. 14)

Strategic analysis entails an examination of a company's external market context and internal factors to determine where the company stands in the market. (p. 18)

Strategic management entails a series of judgments, under uncertainty, that companies direct towards achieving specific goals. (p. 9)

Time-and-motion studies are used to determine how long it takes employees to perform their duties. (p. 7)

Welfare practices were generous endeavors undertaken by some employers, motivated partly out of their motives to minimize employees' desires to seek union representation, promote good management, and to enhance worker productivity. (p. 8)

CHAPTER 1 REVIEW

Fill in the Blanks

Fill in the blanks with the letter of the appropriate terms.

A. Seniority pay
B. Scientific management
C. Line
D. Welfare practices
E. Human capital
F. Layoff
G. Task Identity
H. COLAs
I. Extrinsic compensation
J. Social Security Act of 1935
K. Intrinsic compensation
L. Pay for time-not-worked
M. Staff
N. Compensation features
O. Internally consistent compensation system

1. _____ are the intrinsic and extrinsic rewards employees receive for performing their jobs.

2. Skills variety, task identity, task significance, autonomy, and feedback are examples of _____ and help employees feel responsibility for the outcomes of their work.

3. The degree to which the job is important to others—both inside and outside the company is called _____.

4. _____ practices promoted labor cost control by replacing inefficient production methods with efficient ones.

5. Increases to an employees base pay that are determined by inflation are called _____.

6. Base pay increases that are determined by an employee's length of service are called _____.

7. The knowledge and skills possessed by a company's employees that generate productive capital are considered the company's _____.

8. Legally required retirement benefits are mandated by the _____.

9. Vacations, holiday, and sick days are examples of _____.

10. Assemblers, production workers, and sales employees are examples of _____ employees.

11. Human resources managers and accountants are examples of _____ employees.

12. _____ includes both monetary and nonmonetary rewards for reaching job performance objectives and learning job-related knowledge and skills.

13. To clearly define the relative value of each job among all its jobs, companies use a(n) _____.

14. _____ were originally designed to minimize employees' desires to seek union representation, promote good management, and enhance worker productivity.

15. A _____ is an involuntary termination due to economic slowdowns or plant closings.

Multiple-Choice Questions

Circle the correct answer for each question.

1. The pay increases that are based on changes in prices and indexed by the consumer price index are called
   A. incentive pay increases.
   B. merit pay increases.
   C. inflation adjustments.
   D. cost-of-living adjustments.

2. What is the phrase used to describe the terms of employment reached between labor and management?
   A. Labor-management relations
   B. Collective bargaining agreement
   C. Labor-management agreement
   D. Salary negotiations

3. Another name for fringe compensation is
   A. employee benefits.
   B. intrinsic compensation.
   C. core compensation.
   D. severance pay.

4. Which pay program rewards excellent past performances, motivates future performance, and helps employers retain valued employees?
   A. Merit pay
   B. Incentive pay
   C. Pay-for-knowledge
   D. Skill-based pay

5. This term is used to represent the pay rate differences for jobs of unequal worth and the framework for recognizing differences in employee contributions.

   A. Job analysis
   B. Strategic analysis
   C. Pay structures
   D. Pay ranges

6. This term is used to describe a company's ability to maintain market share and profitability.

   A. Tactical advantage
   B. Strategic advantage
   C. Compensation advantage
   D. Competitive advantage

7. Another name for benefits such as protection programs, pay for time-not-worked, and services is

   A. legally required benefits.
   B. protection benefits.
   C. discretionary benefits.
   D. incentive benefits.

8. To determine whether jobs are equal, the courts of law will look at (a) the skill level needed and how much effort is required to do the job, (b) the amount of responsibility that goes with the position, and (c) the conditions the employee must work under. These are called

   A. compensation factors.
   B. commendable factors.
   C. consideration factors.
   D. compensable factors.

9. What is the other name for compensation, other than base wages or salaries, that fluctuates according to employees' attainment of some standard based on a preestablished formula, individual or group goals, or company earnings?

   A. Merit pay
   B. Incentive pay
   C. Pay-for-knowledge
   D. Skill-based pay

10. Which of the following is **not** considered a core compensation?

    A. Severance pay
    B. Incentive pay
    C. Base pay
    D. Merit pay

11. Through formal education, training, and on-the-job experience, employees can increase their productive value to the company. The abilities of a company's employees are called the their

    A. human resources.
    B. human assets.
    C. human capitol.
    D. human factors.

12. According to the *job characteristics theory*, the five core job dimensions—skill variety, task identity, task significance, autonomy and feedback—are important components of what kind of company compensation plan?

    A. External
    B. Extrinsic
    C. Intrinsic
    D. Internal

13. Which of the following is not one of the three main objectives of a company's compensation system?

    A. Internal consistency
    B. Reducing production overhead
    C. Market competitiveness
    D. Recognizing individual contributions

14. The amount of freedom, independence, and discretion the employee enjoys in determining how to do a job is called

    A. task variety.
    B. freelancing.
    C. skill variety.
    D. autonomy.

15. This compensation plan is designed to encourage employees with a lot of seniority to accept voluntary termination.

    A. Severance pay
    B. Pension program
    C. Early retirement program
    D. Early pension program

Computer Exercise 1

Costing Pay Increases

Pizza Joe's has 2,000 employees and realized a net profit of 10 million dollars last year. Although management is optimistic that profits will continue to grow, they want to maintain control over rising labor costs. This year management expects to spend 60 million dollars on direct payroll costs of wages and salaries, 23 million on "fringe" compensation of legally required and discretionary benefits, for a total payroll and benefit cost of 83 million dollars. These costs represent a significant portion of Pizza Joe's total costs and are expected to continue to rise even if the number of employees remains stable. Pizza Joe's uses a wide variety of pay programs tailored to specific segments of its employee population. They expect costs to rise due to cost-of-living adjustments (COLA), merit pay increases, and incentive pay. All of these increases are expected to be equal to or greater than the consumer price index (CPI), but they can only estimate how much the CPI is likely to grow. As a new Compensation Specialist for Pizza Joe's, you have been asked to estimate the increases in labor costs over the next three years.

Questions

Use the computer calculator to answer these questions, record your answers on the Answer Sheets, and print the entire exercise when your are finished.

1. Determine what the costs of direct payroll and benefits will be during the next three years under the conditions described below.
    - A. If direct payroll and benefits costs both increase by 3% per year, e.g. $83 million X 1.03.
    - B. If direct payroll and benefits costs both increase by 4% per year.
    - C. If direct payroll and benefits costs both increase by 5% per year.

2. In question 1A direct payroll and benefits costs both increased by 3% per year for three years. Use your answer from question 1A to answer these questions.
    - A. How much larger are total payroll (payroll plus benefits) costs after three years than in the beginning (New cost - 83 million)?
    - B. What is the percentage increase in total payroll costs (increase/83 million)?

3. Using your answers from question 1C, determine what would happen to Pizza Joe's profits if all revenue and costs remained the same over the next 3 years **except** for payroll costs and benefits.
    - A. How much larger are total payroll costs after 1 year (New cost - 83 million)?

B. What are Pizza Joe's profits at the end of the above year (10 million - increased costs)?
C. How much larger are total payroll costs after 3 years?
D. What are Pizza Joe's profits at the end of 3 years (10 million - increased costs)?

Further Study

Use the computer calculator to answer these questions, record your answers on the Answer Sheets, and print the entire exercise when your are finished.

F1. Determine what the average annual earnings will be in each of the next 2 years for each of these groups of employees under the conditions below. Mid-level managers, currently average $75,000 per year, Human Resource Specialists currently average $33,000 per year, and Pizza Makers currently average $9.50 per hour ($19,760 per year).
   A. Each groups' average salary increases by 5% per year.
   B. Mid-level managers' average salary increases by 6% per year, Human Resource Specialists' average increases by 4%, and Pizza Makers' average increases by 2%.

CHAPTER 2
Strategic Compensation in Action: Strategic Analysis and Contextual Factors

Learning Objectives

1. Strategic analysis factors
2. Industry classification: North American Industry Classification System (NAICS)
3. External market aspects of strategic analysis
4. Internal capabilities dimensions of strategic analysis
5. Factors that influence companies' competitive strategies and compensation practices

Chapter Outline

I. **Strategic Analysis**

II. **External Market Environment**

III. **Internal Capabilities**

IV. **Factors That Influence Companies' Competitive Strategies and Compensation Practices**
   A. National Culture
   B. Organizational Culture
   C. Organizational and Product Life Cycles

Key Terms

Capital requirements include automated manufacturing technology, and office and plant facilities (p. 31).

Electronic business (e-business) is any process that a business organization conducts over a computer-mediated network. (p. 30)

Electronic commerce (e-commerce) is any transaction completed over a computer-mediated network. (p. 30)

Individualism-collectivism, a dimension of national culture, is the extent to which individuals value personal independence versus group membership. (p. 32)

Industry represents the least broad (that is, the most specific) classification of an industry within the North American Industry Classification System. (p. 24)

Industry group is the fourth most broad classification of industries within the North American Industry Classification System. (p. 24)

Industry profiles describe such basic industry characteristics such as sales volume, pertinent government regulations, and technological advances. (p. 26)

Labor market assessments enable companies to determine the availability of qualified employees. (p. 27)

Masculinity-femininity, a dimension of national culture, refers to whether masculine or feminine values are dominant in society. Masculinity favors material possessions. Femininity encourages caring and nurturing behaviors. (p. 33)

National culture refers to the set of shared norms and beliefs among individuals within national boundaries who are indigenous to that area. (p. 31)

North American Industry Classification System (NAICS) classifies industries using a number system that is used to assist companies in their strategic analyses. (p. 23)

Operating requirements encompass all human resources programs.

Organizational and product life cycles describe the evolution of company and product change using human life cycle stages. Much like people are born, grow, mature, decline, and die; so do companies, products, and services. Business priorities including HR vary with life cycle. (p. 37)

Power distance, a dimension of national culture, is the extent to which people accept a hierarchical system or power structure in companies. (p. 32)

Sector is the broadest classification of industries within the North American Industry Classification System. (p. 24)

Subsector is the second broadest classification of industries within the North American Industry Classification System. (p.24)

Uncertainty avoidance, a dimension of national culture, represents the method by which society deals with risk and instability for its members. (p. 32)

CHAPTER 2 REVIEW

Fill in the Blanks

Fill in the blanks with the letter of the appropriate terms.

A. External elements
B. Functional capabilities
C. National culture
D. Individualistic
E. e-business
F. Internal factors
G. National culture

H. e-commerce
I. Power distance
J. Organizational
K. Scientific management
L. Differentiation
M. Labor market assessments
N. Competitive strategy
O. Uncertainty avoidance

1. Power distance, individualism-collectivism, uncertainty avoidance, and masculinity-femininity are all part of a(n) _____.

2. _____ cultures place value on personal goals, independence, and privacy.

3. _____ is the term for controlling labor costs by improving the efficiency of production methods.

4. _____ is any process that a business conducts over a computer-mediated network.

5. Industry profile, competition, and foreign demand are three of the _____ of a strategic analysis.

6. _____ is any transaction completed over a computer-mediated network.

7. For multinational corporations to develop and maintain a competitive advantage in foreign countries, each country's _____ must be taken into consideration when developing market strategies and employee compensation programs.

8. _____ is a term used to describe a company's effort to remove layers of bureaucracy.

9. In order to promote and sustain a competitive advantage, management uses a(n) _____ to determine how to best utilize their company's resources.

10. Human resources, marketing, and management information systems are examples of the _____ that are keys to maintaining competitive advantage.

11. _____ strategies lead to competitive advantage by developing the unique goods or services that help build brand loyalty.

12. _____ represents the method members of a society use to deal with risk.

13. _____ is the extent that employees accept the hierarchical system in a company.

14. _____ are the financial conditions and functional capabilities that are a part of strategic analysis.

15. _____ are used to determine the availability of qualified job applicants.

Multiple-Choice Questions

Circle the correct answer for each question.

1. Which strategy becomes the focus when companies in the decline phase choose to redirect activities toward distinguishing themselves from the competition by modifying existing products or services or by developing new products or services?
   A. Strategic strategy
   B. Tactical strategy
   C. Competitive strategy
   D. Differentiation strategy

2. These types of companies tend to emphasize market-competitive pay systems over internally consistent ones.
   A. Mature
   B. Growth
   C. Declining
   D. Stabilized

3. Which of the following is an organizational trend toward flatter, less-hierarchical corporate structures that emphasize teamwork over individual contributions alone?
   A. Downsizing
   B. Two-tier reorganization
   C. Recertification
   D. Broadbanding

4. To maintain market share, which of the following is recommended for mature companies?
   A. Differentiation strategies
   B. Long-term incentive strategies
   C. Lowest cost strategies
   D. Short-term incentive strategies

5. Foreign demand, competition, and industry profile are three of the five elements of this part of conducting a strategic analysis.
   A. Functional capabilities
   B. Labor market assessments
   C. Internal factors
   D. External market environment

6. Most companies that are in their organizational growth phase tend to use this type of pay system.
   A. Internally consistent
   B. Market-competitive
   C. Merit
   D. Two-tier

7. Which strategy refers to the planned use of a company's resources to develop and maintain an advantage in the marketplace?
   A. Strategic strategy
   B. Differentiation strategy
   C. Competitive strategy
   D. Tactical strategy

8. Which of the following is **not** considered a company resource?
   A. Capital
   B. Training
   C. Technology
   D. Human resources

9. Differentiation strategies are most appropriate in which phase of the organizational life cycle?
   A. Maturity phase
   B. Growth phase
   C. Threat phase
   D. Decline phase

10. When companies do this, they generally change to use only a few large salary ranges that will span previously used pay grades.
    A. Broadbanding
    B. Uncertainty avoidance
    C. Competitive strategizing
    D. Financial restructuring

11. Which strategy depends on employee creativity, openness to novel work approaches, and willingness to take risks?
    A. Strategic strategy
    B. Differentiation strategy
    C. Competitive strategy
    D. Tactical strategy

12. Low-cost strategies are most appropriate for companies in which phase of their organizational life cycle?
    A. Maturity phase
    B. Growth phase
    C. Threat phase
    D. Decline phase

13. This type of culture is determined by the shared values and beliefs that set a workplace's behavioral norms.
    A. Traditional
    B. Societal
    C. National
    D. Organizational

14. In the *North American Industry Classification System* five-digit classification code, the first two digits stand for which of the following?
    A. Industry
    B. Subsector
    C. Sector
    D. Group

15. The company's financial condition and functional capabilities are part of which step in strategic analysis?
    A. External market context
    B. Internal factors
    C. Strategic factors
    D. Industry profiles

CHAPTER 2 REVIEW

Fill-in the Blanks

Fill in the blanks with the letter of the appropriate key terms.

A.	welfare practices programs		H.	compensation
B.	strategic decisions		I.	cost leadership
C.	national culture		J.	organizational management
D.	individualist		K.	scientific
E.	tactical		L.	differentiation
F.	piecework plans		M.	collectiveness
G.	administrative		N.	competitive strategy
			O.	time-and-motion studies

1. _____ is the term for controlling labor costs by improving the efficiency of production methods.

2. Compensation changed from an _____ to a strategic function of management.

3. In order to determine how long it takes employees to complete certain tasks, management uses _____.

4. _____ are compensation practices that pay employees for the number of units they produce over a specific period of time.

5. Management might institute certain types of _____ in order to avoid employee unionization.

6. In the early 1980's, designing and implementing _____ transformed personnel administration from a largely administrative function to management function used to contribute to the company's competitive advantage.

7. _____ decisions are required to guide the activities of management in order to reach specific marketing goals.

8. In order to promote and sustain a competitive advantage, management uses a _____ to determine how to best utilize their company's resources.

9. _____ decisions are used to support competitive strategy practices.

10. _____ strategy describes management's efforts to produce and sell its company's goods or services at a price advantage relative to the industry average.

11. _____ strategies lead to competitive advantage by developing the unique goods or services that help build brand loyalty.

12. For multinational corporations to develop and maintain a competitive advantage in foreign countries, each country's _____ must be taken into consideration when developing market strategies and employee compensation programs.

13. _____ cultures favor social cohesiveness and loyalty among fellow employees.

14. _____ cultures place value on personal goals, independence, and privacy.

15. _____ culture is the shared values and beliefs that produce the norms of behavior within a company.

Multiple Choice Questions

Circle the correct answer for each question.

1. Which of the following is **not** an example of a company's welfare compensation practice?
    - A. library facilities
    - B. recreational center
    - C. food stamps
    - D. financial aid for education

2. Which of the following is **not** considered a company resource?
    - A. capital
    - B. training
    - C. technology
    - D. human resources

3. Which strategy refers to the planned use of a company's resources to develop and maintain an advantage in the marketplace?
    - A. strategic strategy
    - B. differentiation strategy
    - C. competitive strategy
    - D. tactical strategy

4. Which strategy depends on employee creativity, openness to novel work approaches, and willingness to take risks?

   A. strategic strategy
   B. differentiation strategy
   C. competitive strategy
   D. tactical strategy

5. Which of the following is an organizational trend toward flatter, less hierarchical corporate structures that emphasize teamwork over individual contributions alone?

   A. down sizing
   B. two-tier reorganization
   C. recertification
   D. broadbanding

6. Differentiation strategies are most appropriate in which phase of the organizational life cycle?

   A. maturity phase
   B. growth phase
   C. threat phase
   D. decline phase

7. Low-cost strategies are most appropriate for companies in which phase of their organizational life-cycle?

   A. maturity phase
   B. growth phase
   C. threat phase
   D. decline phase

8. Which strategy becomes the focus when companies in the decline phase, choose to redirect activities toward distinguishing themselves from the competition by modifying existing products or services or by developing new products or services?

   A. strategic strategy
   B. differentiation strategy
   C. competitive strategy
   D. tactical strategy

9. This term is used to refer to the activities performed when one summarizes a job's purpose and list the tasks, duties, and responsibilities, as well as the skills, knowledge
and abilities necessary to perform the job adequately.

   A. job content
   B. job analysis
   C. job description
   D. job appraisal

10. When high-performing employees voluntarily terminate their employment and subsequently go to work for a competitor company its called what kind of turnover?

    A. disparate turnover
    B. diversified turnover
    C. demeaning turnover
    D. dysfunctional turnover

11. In compensation practices, this term refers to employees' beliefs about the appropriateness of the <u>policies</u> and <u>practices</u> used to determine pay and pay-increase amounts.

    A. procedural fairness
    B. distributive fairness
    C. compensation fairness
    D. pay scale fairness

12. In compensation practices, this term refers to employees' beliefs about the appropriateness of the <u>actual</u> pay and pay-increase amounts.

    A. procedural fairness
    B. distributive fairness
    C. compensation fairness
    D. pay scale fairness

13. This strategy describes management's efforts to develop and market its company's goods or services at the lowest price.

    A. tactical strategy
    B. strategic strategy
    C. competitive strategy
    D. cost-leadership strategy

14. To reach its marketing goals, these type of decisions must be made to direct the activities of a company's management team.
    - A. tactical decisions
    - B. strategic decisions
    - C. scientific decisions
    - D. competitive decisions

15. Most companies that are in their organizational growth phase tend to use this type of pay system.
    - A. internally consistent
    - B. market-competitive
    - C. merit
    - D. two-tier

Computer Exercise 2

Compensation System Review

The Director of Compensation has asked you to conduct a portion of this year's compensation system review. Specifically, you are to evaluate the pilot "retention program" that was implemented at Pizza Joe's Illinois Plant one year ago. You learn that two years ago the Illinois plant was experiencing dysfunctional turnover among management employees. Although Pizza Joe's management turnover averages about 5% per year, this plant had lost 4 out of 20 management employees in one year. All of the employees had reported that they quit to take higher paying jobs and they all were among the plant's best performers. It cost over $28,000 in recruitment expenses to replace these 4 employees. The plant experienced a decline in productivity that year which was estimated to have reduced company profits by $200,000.

The Plant Manager attributed the decline in productivity to the problems arising from turnover and successfully argued to implement a "retention program" in which he received a pool of $10,000 to distribute as lump sum bonuses. He was allowed to make these awards in any equitable basis he chose. At the end of the pilot year, productivity had returned to target levels, but 2 solid performers quit after failing to receive bonuses. The Recruiter estimates that it will cost about $14,000 in recruitment expenses to replace these two employees ($7,000 a piece). The Plant Manager is asking for another pool of $10,000 to continue the retention program. The Director of Compensation has asked for your recommendation.

Questions

Use the computer calculator to answer these questions, record your answers on the Answer Sheets, and then print your answers.

1. According to this Plant Manager, how much did the turnover of 4 employees cost the firm? Include recruitment costs and lost profits.

2. If the implementation of the retention program cut the costs from question 1 in half, how much money was saved after subtracting the $10,000 price of the program?

3. The savings in question 2 were generated by a program for only 20 management employees. How much could Pizza Joe's save by implementing this program for 200 management employees?

Further Study

F1. Assume that the original resignations were not pay related and that the retention program actually **increased** turnover from the normal 5% (1 person) to 10% (2 people). Follow these steps to calculate the total costs of the program.
    A.   What is the cost of recruiting one more person?
    B.   What is the direct cost of the retention program?
    C.   What is the loss of profits (200,000/4)?
    D.   What is the total cost of the retention program (A + B + C)?

F2. The above costs were generated by a program for only 20 management employees. How much could Pizza Joe's lose by implementing this program for 200 management employees?

CHAPTER 3

Contextual Influences on Compensation Practice

Learning Objectives

1. Compensation and the social good
2. Various laws that influence private sector companies' and labor unions' compensation practices.
3. Contextual influences on the federal government's compensation practices
4. Labor unions' influence on companies' compensation practices
5. Market factors' impact on companies' compensation practices

Chapter Outline

I. **Compensation and the Social Good**

II. **Employment Laws That Influence Compensation Practices**
   A. Income Continuity, Safety, and Work Hours
   B. Pay Discrimination
   C. Accommodating Disabilities and Family Needs
   D. Prevailing Wage Laws

III. **Contextual Influences on the Federal Government as an Employer**
   A. Labor Unions as Contextual Influences
   B. National Labor Relations Act of 1935
   C. Compensation Issues in Collective Bargaining
   D. Market Influences

Key Terms

Aaron v. City of Wichita, Kansas is a court ruling that offered several criteria to determine whether City of Wichita fire chiefs are exempt employees, including the relative importance of management as opposed to other duties, frequency with which they exercise discretionary powers, relative freedom from supervision, and the relationship between their salaries and wages paid to other employees for similar nonexempt work. (p. 49)

Affirmative action refers to the attempt to promote the employment of individuals who are protected under the Civil Rights Act of 1964. (p. 54)

Americans with Disabilities Act of 1990 (ADA) prohibits discrimination against individuals with mental or physical disabilities. (p. 57)

Bennett Amendment to Title VII of the Civil Rights Act allows employees to charge employers with Title VII violations. (p. 53)

Civil Rights Act of 1964, specifically Title VII, was enacted to promote equal employment opportunities for underrepresented minorities. (p. 50)

Civil Rights Act of 1991 shifted the burden of proof in workplace discrimination from the employees to the employers and extends protection to Senate employees and political appointees. (p. 55)

Comparable worth refers to jobs that are similar but not equal and is an issue in setting pay rates. (p. 52)

Compensable factors, which are skill, effort, responsibility, and working conditions, are used to set pay rates. (p. 51)

Concessionary bargaining refers to union contract negotiations that focus more on job security than higher wages. (p. 61)

Davis-Bacon Act of 1931 established employment standards for federal construction contractors with contracts over $2,000. (p. 58)

Disparate impact represents unintentional discrimination due to unequal treatment for an employee who is part of a protected group. (p. 53)

Disparate treatment represents intentional discrimination by employers that is based on an employee's race, color, gender, national origin, or religion. (p. 53)

Equal Pay Act of 1963 prohibits sex discrimination in pay. (p. 50)

Executive Order 11246 requires companies holding contracts (worth more than $50,000 per year and employing 50 or more employees) with the federal government develop written affirmative action plans each year. (p. 54)

Exempt refers to an employee's status regarding the overtime pay provision of the Fair Labor Standards Act of 1938 (FLSA, see below). Generally, administrative, professional, and executive employees are exempt from the FLSA overtime and minimum wage provisions. (p. 48)

Fair Labor Standards Act of 1938 (FLSA) addresses major abuses that intensified during the Great Depression and the transition from agricultural to industrial enterprises. These include substandard pay, excessive work hours, and the employment of children in oppressive working conditions. (p. 46)

Family and Medical Leave Act of 1993 (FMLA) allows employees protection from job discrimination while off work to care for family members or while ill themselves. (p. 58)

McNamara-O'Hara Service Contract Act of 1965 requires contractors of service workers to pay the local prevailing wages. (p. 50)

National Labor Relations Act of 1935 (NLRA) was enacted to remove barriers to free commerce and to restore equality of bargaining power between employees and employers. (p. 59)

Nonexempt refers to an employee's status regarding the overtime pay provision of the Fair Labor Standards Act of 1938 (FLSA). Generally, employees whose jobs do not fall into particular categories (that is, administrative, professional, and executive employees) are covered by overtime and minimum wage provisions. (p. 49)

Older Workers Benefit Protection Act (OWBPA) is the 1990 amendment to ADEA that placed restrictions on employers' benefits practices. (p. 55)

Portal-to-Portal Act of 1947 defines the term "hours worked" that appears in the FLSA. (p. 49)

Pregnancy Discrimination Act of 1978 provides workplace discrimination protection for pregnant employees. (p. 57)

Social Security Act of 1935 was enacted in response to the Great Depression to provide temporary income to workers who were unemployed. (p. 46)

Spillover effect refers to the indirect influences union contracts have on nonunion compensation amounts. (p. 60)

Walsh-Healey Public Contracts Act of 1936 covers contractors who sell supplies, materials, or equipment over $10,000 to the federal government. (p. 58)

CHAPTER 3 REVIEW

Fill in the Blanks

Fill in the blanks with the appropriate terms.

A. Pay discrimination
B. Poverty threshold
C. Government
D. EEOC
E. Responsibility
F. Market shares
G. Minimum wage
H. Employment discrimination
I. Social good
J. Judicial
K. Child labor provisions
L. Divisions of labor within factories
M. Federal
N. Department of Labor
O. Job Security

1. Four factors the federal government uses to define *compensable factors* are: The skill level need to perform the job; the amount of mental or physical effort that must be expended to perform the job; the conditions the job will have to be performed; and the amount of _____ the employee is given to perform the job.

2. These three factors led to the federal government passing laws concerning income continuity, safety, and work hours: the move from family businesses to large factories, the *Great Depression,* and _____.

3. The three branches of the federal government are the executive, legislative, and _____.

4. _____ was implemented to insure a minimally acceptable standard of living for workers.

5. The fundamental goal of most employees is to attain high wages, comprehensive benefits, safe and healthy working conditions, and _____.

6. Congress enacted the Equal Pay Act of 1963 to remedy a serious problem of _____ in private industry.

7. Federal compensation laws are grouped according to these four themes: Income, continuity, _____, accommodating disabilities and family needs, and prevailing wage laws.

8. Private sector employers strive to increase profits, _____, and returns on investment.

9. The Fair Labor Standards Act of 1938 addressed these three broad issues: Minimum wage, overtime pay, and _____.

10. Most of the laws that influence compensation practices were established at the _____ level of government.

11. Three factions have a direct effect on a citizen's ability to participate as consumers in the economy. They are employees, employers, and _____.

12. _____ is given the responsibility of investigating and reconciling charges of illegal discrimination.

13. _____ represents the minimum annual earnings needed to afford housing and to meet other basic needs.

14. When the economy is booming, unemployment is low, wages and benefits are progressive, and the working conditions are safe. This is called _____.

15. Exemptions to the minimum wage laws must be approved by the _____.

Multiple-Choice Questions

Circle the correct answer for each question.

1. The Pregnancy Discrimination Act of 1978 protected all of the following rights for pregnancy-related reasons **except**
   A. paid time off.
   B. credit for previous service.
   C. accrued retirement benefits.
   D. accumulated seniority.

2. This 1963 act was based on the principle that men and women should receive the same pay when they are performing substantially similar jobs.
   A. Equal Pay Act
   B. Davis-Bacon Act
   C. McNamara-O'Hara Service Contract Act
   D. Work Hours and Safety Standards Act

3. The Age Discrimination in Employment Act protects workers from illegal age discrimination starting at age
   A. 60.
   B. 50.
   C. 40.
   D. 55.

4. This federal act, passed in 1947, defined the term *hours worked*.
   A. Fair Labor Standards Act
   B. Social Security Act
   C. Portal-to-Portal Act
   D. Civil Rights Act

5. When union officials switched the emphasis in contract negotiations from seeking substantial wage increases to job security issues, this was called what kind of bargaining?
   A. Collective
   B. Conciliatory
   C. Compensatory
   D. Concessionary

6. One of the main provisions of this 1965 act was to require contractors, with government contracts to pay local prevailing wages.
   A. Equal Pay Act
   B. Davis-Bacon Act
   C. McNamara-O'Hara Service Contract Act
   D. Work Hours and Safety Standards Act

7. The purposes of this act were to remove barriers to free commerce and to institute equality of bargaining power between employees and employers.
   A. Walsh-Healy Act
   B. National Labor Relations Act
   C. The Collective Bargaining Act
   D. Fair Labor Standards Act

8. In 1964, the federal government passed this act in order to protect workers from discriminatory employment decisions.
   A. Fair Labor Standards Act
   B. Social Security Act
   C. Portal-to-Portal Act
   D. Civil Rights Act

9. When some workers are treated less favorably than others because of their race, color, gender, national origin, or religion, it is called what type of intentional discrimination?
   A. Incomparable worth
   B. Disparate impact
   C. The glass ceiling effect
   D. Disparate treatment

10. Which of the following could be considered a business with a high degree of capital intensity?
    A. Banking
    B. Stock market trading
    C. Manufacturing
    D. Export trading

11. This form of unintentional discrimination occurs whenever an employer applies an employment practice to all employees, but it leads to unequal treatment of protected employee groups.
    A. Incomparable worth
    B. Disparate impact
    C. The glass ceiling effect
    D. Disparate treatment

12. This 1935 federal act provided temporary income to workers who were chronically unemployed due to the Great Depression.
    A. Fair Labor Standards Act
    B. Social Security Act
    C. Portal-to-Portal Act
    D. Civil Rights Act

13. Artificial barriers that prevent qualified minority men and women from advancing to and reaching their full career potential are called
    A. disparate treatment.
    B. disparate impact.
    C. incomparable worth.
    D. glass ceiling.

14. Because factory owners were paying employees low wages, making them work in unsafe working conditions, and taking advantage of their employees in other ways, the federal government, in 1938, passed the following act.
    A. Fair Labor Standards Act
    B. Social Security Act
    C. Portal-to-Portal Act
    D. Civil Rights Act

15. This act was passed in 1962 requiring contractors to pay employees time and one-half for any hours worked over 40 in one week.
    A. Equal Pay Act
    B. Davis-Bacon Act
    C. McNamara-O'Hara Service Contract Act
    D. Work Hours and Safety Standards Act

Computer Exercise 3

Responding to Alleged Pay Discrimination

Sue Jones, an engineer at Pizza Joe's, alleges that female engineers are being paid less than male engineers due to their sex. You have been asked to gather salary data from the engineering work group to help investigate this allegation. You compile the data below, including current performance ratings, for all the engineers in the same pay level. Note that all the engineers initially joined your firm as inexperienced trainees with Bachelors' degrees. You know that Pizza Joe's uses a merit pay system with the following performance ratings: Outstanding (5), Excels (4), Satisfactory (3), Needs Improvement (2), and Unsatisfactory (1). The salary range for this pay level is $3,280 to $4,920 per month.

Name	Sex	Race	Tenure	Ratings	Monthly Salary
Cruz	M	Hispanic	9	4	$4,600
Duncan	M	White	9	3	$4,400
Fry	M	White	8	3	$4,250
Smith	M	Black	8	3	$4,100
Ward	M	White	5	4	$4,150
Saul	M	White	5	3	$4,100
Pena	F	White	5	5	$4,300
Lucas	M	White	4	3	$4,000
Hollis	F	White	4	3	$4,000
Jones*	F	Black	4	2	$3,800

*Complainant

Questions

Use the computer calculator to answer theses questions, record your answers on the Answer Sheets, and then print your answers.

1. What is the average salary of the males versus the females including complainant and excluding complainant? To calculate averages sum the salaries and divide by the number of salaries in the total.

2. What is the average tenure for the males versus the females including and excluding the complainant?

3. What is the average performance rating for the males versus the females including and excluding the complainant?

4. A. What is the average salary of males versus females for those employees with 5 or fewer years of tenure including and excluding complainant?
   B. What are the average performance ratings for these same groups?

Further Study

Record your written responses on the Answer Sheets and print.

F1. Based on the data, what factors other than sex may explain pay differences?

F2. Does your review support Sue Jone's allegation of sex discrimination? Use data to support your conclusion. Is further investigation of pay discrimination needed? If yes, why?

CHAPTER 4
Traditional Bases for Pay: Seniority and Merit

Learning Objectives

1. U.S. business' traditional practice of setting employees' base pay on their seniority or longevity with the company
2. The fit of seniority pay practices with the two competitive strategies—lowest cost and differentiation
3. U.S. business' traditional practice of setting employees' base pay on their merit
4. The role of performance appraisal in the merit pay process
5. Ways to strengthen the pay-for-performance link
6. Some possible limitations of merit pay programs
7. How merit pay programs fit with the two competitive strategies—lowest cost and differentiation

Chapter Outline

I. **Seniority or Longevity Pay**
   A. Historical Overview
   B. Who Participates
   C. Effectiveness of Seniority Pay Systems
   D. Design of Seniority Pay and Longevity Pay Plans
   E. Advantages of Seniority Pay
   F. Fitting Seniority Pay with Competitive Strategies

II. **Merit Pay**
   A. Who Participates?
   B. Exploring the Elements of Merit Pay

III. **Performance Appraisal**
   A. Types of Performance Appraisal Plans
   B. Exploring the Performance Appraisal Process

IV. Strengthening the Pay-for-Performance Link
   A. Link Performance Appraisals to Business Goals
   B. Communication
   C. Establish Effective Appraisals
   D. Empower Employees
   E. Differentiate among Performers

V. Possible Limitations of Merit Pay Programs
   A. Failure to Differentiate among Performers
   B. Poor Performance Measures
   C. Supervisors' Biased Ratings of Employee Job Performance
   D. Lack of Open Communication Between Management and Employees
   E. Undesirable Social Structures
   F. Factors Other Than Merit
   G. Undesirable Competition
   H. Little Motivational Value

VI. Linking Merit Pay with Competitive Strategy
   A. Lowest-Cost Competitive Strategy
   B. Differentiation Competitive Strategy

Key Terms

Behaviorally anchored rating scales (BARS), a specific kind of behavioral system, is based on the critical incident technique, and these scales are developed in the same fashion with one exception. For the CIT, a critical incident would be written as "the incumbent completed the task in a timely fashion." For the BARS format, this incident would be written as "the incumbent is expected to complete the task in a timely fashion." (p. 76)

Behavioral observation scale (BOS), a specific kind of behavioral system, displays illustrations of positive incidents (or behaviors) of job performance for various job dimensions. The evaluator rates the employee on each behavior according to the extent to which the employee performs in a manner consistent with each behavioral description. (p. 78)

Behavioral systems, a type of performance appraisal method, requires that raters (for example, supervisors) judge the extent to which employees display successful job performance behaviors. (p. 76)

Bias errors occur when the rater evaluates the employees based on the rater's negative or positive opinion of the employees rather than the employees' performances. (p. 81)

***Brito* v. *Zia Company*,** a Supreme Court ruling, deemed that the Zia Company violated Title VII of the Civil Rights Act of 1964 when a disproportionate number of protected class individuals were laid off on the basis of low performance appraisal scores. Zia Company's action was a violation of Title VII because the use of the performance appraisal system in determining layoffs was indeed an employment test. In addition, the court ruled that the Zia Company had not demonstrated that its performance appraisal instrument was valid. (p. 79)

Comparison systems are a type of performance appraisal method that requires that raters (for example, supervisors) evaluate a given employee's performance against other employees' performance attainments. Employees are ranked from the best performer to the poorest performer. (p. 74)

Contrast errors occur when a rater (for example, a supervisor) compares an employee to other employees rather than to specific, explicit performance standards. (p. 82)

Critical incident technique (CIT) is a specific kind of behavioral system that requires job incumbents and their supervisors to identify performance incidents—on-the-job behaviors and behavioral outcomes—that distinguish successful performance from unsuccessful performance. The supervisor then observes the employees and records their performance on these critical job aspects. (p. 76)

Errors of central tendency occur when raters (for example, supervisors) judge all employees as average or close to average. (p. 82)

First-impression effect occurs when a rater (for example, a supervisor) makes an initial favorable or unfavorable judgment about an employee, and then ignores or distorts the employee's actual performance based on this impression. (p. 81)

Forced distribution is a specific kind of comparison performance appraisal system in which raters (for example, supervisors) assign employees to groups that represent the entire range of performance. (p. 74)

General Schedule (GS) classifies federal government jobs into 15 classifications (GS-1 through GS-15) based on such factors as skill, education, and experience levels. In addition, jobs that require high levels of specialized education (for example, a physicist), influence significantly on public policy (for example, law judges), or require executive decision making are classified into three additional categories: Senior level (SL), Scientific & Professional (ST) positions, and the Senior Executive Service (SES). (p. 69)

Illegal discriminatory bias occurs when a supervisor rates members of his or her race, gender, nationality, or religion more favorably than members of other classes. (p. 82)

Job control unionism refers to a union's success in negotiating formal contracts with employees and establishing quasi-judicial grievance procedures to adjudicate disputes between union members and employers. (p. 67)

Just-meaningful pay increase refers to the minimum pay increase that employees will see as making a substantial change in compensation. (p. 72)

Leniency errors occur when raters (for example, supervisors) appraise an employee's performance more highly than what it really rates compared to objective criteria. (p. 82)

Management by objectives (MBO), a goal-oriented performance appraisal method, requires that supervisors and employees determine objectives for employees to meet during the rating period, and the employees appraise how well they have achieved their objectives. (p. 78)

Merit bonus (nonrecurring merit increases) are lump sum monetary awards based on employees' past performance. Employees do not continue to receive nonrecurring merit increases every year. Instead, employees must earn them each time. (p. 86)

Merit pay programs reward employees with permanent increases to base pay according to differences in job performance. (p. 71)

Negative halo effect occurs when a rater (for example, a supervisor) generalizes an employee's negative behavior on one aspect of the job to all aspects of the job. (p. 82)

Paired comparisons, a variation of simple ranking job evaluation plans, orders all jobs from lowest to highest based on comparing the worth of each job in all possible job pairs. Paired comparison also refers to a specific kind of comparison method for appraising job performance. Supervisors compare each employee to every other employee, identifying the better performer in each pair. (p. 75)

Positive halo effect occurs when a rater (for example, a supervisor) generalizes employees' positive behavior on one aspect of the job to all aspects of the job. (p. 82)

Rating errors in performance appraisal reflect differences between human judgment processes versus objective, accurate assessments uncolored by bias, prejudice, or other subjective, extraneous influences. (p. 81)

Seniority pay (longevity pay) systems reward employees with permanent additions to base pay periodically according to employees' length of service performing their jobs. (p. 66)

Similar-to-me effect refers to the tendency on the part of raters (for example, supervisors) to favorably judge employees whom they perceive as similar to themselves. (p. 82)

Strictness errors occur when raters (for example, supervisors) judge employee performance to be less than what it compares against objective criteria. (p. 82)

Trait systems, a type of performance appraisal method, requires raters (for example, supervisors or customers) to evaluate each employee's traits or characteristics such as quality of work, quantity of work, appearance, dependability, cooperation, initiative, judgment, leadership responsibility, decision-making ability, or creativity. (p. 73)

CHAPTER 4 REVIEW

Fill in the Blanks

Fill in the blanks with the appropriate terms.

A. Longevity
B. Job design
C. Comparison system
D. Job analysis
E. Rating errors
F. Forced distribution
G. Merit pay
H. Management by objectives
I. Inflation
J. Seniority
K. Just-meaningful pay increase
L. Trait system
M. Job control unionism
N Paired comparison
O. General Schedule

1. The _____ performance appraisal system is used to evaluate such things as quality of work, personal appearance, dependability, and initiative.

2. A compensation program that rewards employees who already have reached their highest pay grade, and therefore receive pay raises based on something other than how long they have been with the company, is called _____ pay.

3. _____ reflect differences between human judgment processes and objectives, accurate assessments uncolored by bias, prejudice, or other subjective, extraneous influences.

4. To determine if a merit pay program is appropriate, compensation professionals should consider two main factors: commitment from top management and _____.

5. In the _____ performance appraisal method, an employee's performance is compared to every other employee, individually, with the amount of compensation increase based on the number of times that employee's performance was rated better than the other employees.

6. _____ classifies federal employees into 15 classifications that determines their base pay amount.

7. _____ refers to the minimum pay increase that employees will see as making a worthwhile change in their base pay.

8. An employee/employer system that uses a collective bargaining unit to negotiate contracts and settle grievances is called _____.

9. _____ programs base employee compensation amounts on job performance as opposed to length of service.

10. When an employee's performance is evaluated and then placed into one of several categories, it is called the _____ appraisal method.

11. Compensating employees because they have been with the same company for a long time and, therefore, are presumed to be more proficient is called _____ pay.

12. _____ is essential for the development of content-valid performance appraisal systems.

13. The _____ performance appraisal system is based on comparing an employee's performance against the performance of other employees.

14. _____ represents rises in the cost of consumer goods and services that boost the overall cost of living.

15. In the _____ performance appraisal technique, both supervisors and employees set performance goals, then the employees evaluate how effective they think they were in meeting those goals.

Multiple-Choice Questions

Circle the correct answer for each question.

1. When an employee levels charges of illegal pay discrimination against an employer, it comes under the guidelines set down in the
    A. Equal Pay Act.
    B. Pay Discrimination Act.
    C. Civil Rights Act.
    D. Fair Labor Standards Act.

2. When an evaluator generalizes a favorable employee behavior on one task to the employee's overall behavior, the employee's rating is subject to which bias error?
    A. Positive halo effect
    B. Similar-to-me effect
    C. Negative halo effect
    D. First-impression effect

3. Most unionized and public sector organizations continue to base an employee's pay on
    A. length of service.
    B. merit.
    C. employee's age.
    D. job performance.

4. This type of bias error in performance appraisal can occur when evaluators rate all employees as average or close to average.
   A. Leniency errors
   B. Strictness errors
   C. Errors of central tendency
   D. Contrast errors

5. The forced distribution performance appraisal method is part of which appraisal system?
   A. Trait
   B. Comparison
   C. Goal-oriented
   D. Competitive

6. Which of the following categories are **not** performance appraisal methods?
   A. Trait systems
   B. Comparison systems
   C. Goal-oriented systems
   D. Competitive systems

7. In this behavioral system technique, employees are evaluated according to the extent to which they perform in a manner consistent with each behavioral description.
   A. Behaviorally anchored rating scale
   B. Behavioral observation
   C. Critical incident
   D. Behavioral incident

8. As a rule, supervisors give merit pay increases to employees on the basis of _____ appraisal of employee performance.
   A. objective
   B. subjective
   C. standard
   D. free-form

9. Basing pay on seniority is a/an _____ type of assessment standard.
   A. objective
   B. subjective
   C. standard
   D. free-form

10. Which of the following is **not** considered a limitation of merit pay programs?
    A. Failure to differentiate among employees
    B. Empowerment of employees
    C. Undesirable competition
    D. Undesirable social structures

11. This form of pay increase refers to the minimum pay increase that employees will see as making a noticeable change in their compensation.
    A. Minimally-meaningful
    B. Cost of living
    C. Minimally acceptable
    D. Just-meaningful

12. This behavioral system technique is the most highly defensible in court because it is based on actual observable job behaviors.
    A. Behaviorally anchored rating scale
    B. Behavioral observation
    C. Critical incident
    D. Behavioral incident

13. Which of the following would **not** strengthen a merit pay program?
    A. Linking performance appraisal to business goals
    B. Performing job analyses
    C. Empowering employees
    D. Not differentiating among employees

14. Perhaps the most effective performance appraisal technique is this technique.
    A. Critical incident
    B. Paired-comparison
    C. Management by objectives
    D. Behavioral observation scale

15. In this *behavioral system technique*, employees and supervisors identify on-the-job behaviors and behavioral outcomes that distinguish successful from unsuccessful performances.
    A. Behaviorally anchored rating scale
    B. Behavioral observation
    C. Critical incident
    D. Behavioral incident

Computer Exercise 4

Comparing the Costs of Merit Pay vs. Merit Bonuses

Pizza Joe's Marketing Department has been chosen to pilot a Merit Bonus Program for clerical positions. These positions are all at the same pay level and the current pay range is $17,000 to $23,800 per year. The current Merit Pay Program awarded the following increases last year based on a performance ratings scale ranging from 1 to 5:

Outstanding (5)	Excels (4)	Satisfactory (3)	Needs Improvement (2)	Unsatisfactory (1)
6%	5%	4%	2%	0%

Merit pay increases combine cost of living adjustments (COLA) and merit into a single raise which averages about 5%. The pilot will give a 3% COLA increase to the clerks with a 3 or better rating, and no increase to those rated less than 3. The manager will use the remaining 2% of the payroll budget for lump sum merit bonuses. Below is a chart that shows the results of **last year's** merit process. The manager is not sure if he should participate in this pilot. He has asked you to develop scenarios on how the pilot might affect the department.

Name	Old Salary	Rating	% Increase	$ Increase	New Salary
Adams	$16,800	3	4%	$672	$17,472
Lee	$17,500	4	5%	$875	$18,375
Smith	$18,000	2	2%	$360	$18,360
Garcia	$18,500	3	4%	$740	$19,240
Cook	$18,500	5	6%	$1,110	$19,610
Day	$19,000	4	5%	$950	$19,950
Brown	$19,500	3	4%	$780	$20,280
Post	$19,500	4	5%	$975	$20,475
Morgan	$20,000	3	4%	$800	$20,800
Fall	$21,500	3	4%	$860	$22,360

Questions

Use the chart in computer exercise 4 software to complete this assignment. Enter the COLA percentage and the computer will calculate what the employees' new base salaries under the pilot Merit Bonus system would be. These salaries are listed in the "New Salary (with COLA)" column. Enter the Merit Bonus budget percentage and the computer will calculate the Merit Bonus budget. Then review the performance ratings and allocate **individual** merit bonuses based on your own judgment. Use the entire Merit Bonus budget by entering a bonus or zero for each employee until the "Used" funds equal the "Total" funds shown on the computer screen.

The computer will add the bonuses you allocate with each employee's "New Salary" to show you the employee's "Total Cash" earnings under the pilot. The computer will also calculate what the employee's base salary would have been under the old merit pay system and list this figure in the column labeled "Merit Salary". This allows you to compare each employee's earnings under the pilot ("Total Cash") with what she/he would have earned under the old merit system "Merit Salary". Complete the exercise and print your answers.

1. Follow these steps to distribute bonuses for the first year of the pilot. Enter a 3% COLA and a 2% Merit Bonus percent on the right hand side of the chart. The computer will calculate the Merit Bonus budget. Review the merit ratings in the chart and use your judgment to allocate individual merit bonuses. Use the entire Merit Bonus budget by entering a bonus or zero for each employee until the "Used" funds equal the "Total" funds shown on the computer screen.

2. Which employees will have higher earnings under the pilot than under the old merit pay system? Lower? Is this desirable? Write your answers on Answer Sheet 2. (Note: Compare each employee's earnings under the pilot ("Total Cash") with what she/he would have earned under the old merit system "Merit Salary".)

3. In year 2, Pizza Joe's decides to allocate 2% to the COLA and 3% to the merit bonus budget. Enter these numbers on the chart and distribute the individual bonuses. Use the entire Merit Bonus budget by entering a bonus or zero for each employee until the "Used" funds equal the "Total" funds shown on the computer screen.

4. For year 3, enter a 2% COLA and a 3% Merit Bonus percent. Then enter new merit ratings, assume that each person's rating goes up by 1, e.g. from a 3 to a 4, up to a maximum of 5. Then distribute bonuses for year 3 of the pilot.

5. Do you think you need any additional information in order to distribute bonuses equitably? Why or why not?

Further Study

Explain your answers on the Answer Sheets.

F1. If the rest of Pizza Joe's is using the old merit pay system, which employees might want to transfer out of the department using the pilot? Would this be beneficial or detrimental to the department?

F2. Based on your analysis do you have any recommendations or changes you would like to see in the pilot? If these involve changes in COLA or the merit bonus budget make the changes in the chart and explain the results.

CHAPTER 5
Incentive Pay

Learning Objectives

1. How incentive pay and traditional pay systems—merit and seniority—differ
2. Plans that reward individual behavior
3. A variety of plans that reward group behavior
4. The most broadly used companywide incentive plan—profit sharing and stock option plans
5. Considerations for designing incentive pay plans
6. How individual, group, and gain sharing incentive plans contribute to differentiation and lowest cost competitive strategies

Chapter Outline

I. Contrasting Incentive Pay with Traditional Pay

II. Individual Incentives
    A. Defining Individual Incentives
    B. Types of Individual Incentive Plans
    C. Advantages of Individual Incentive Pay Programs
    D. Disadvantages of Individual Incentive Pay Programs

III. Group Incentives
    A. Defining Group Incentives
    B. Types of Group Incentive Plans
    C. Advantages of Group Incentives
    D. Disadvantages of Group Incentives

IV. Companywide Incentives
    A. Defining Companywide Incentives
    B. Types of Companywide Incentives
    C. Profit Sharing Plans
    D. Employee Stock Option Plans

V. Designing Incentive Pay Programs
    A. Group versus Individual Incentives
    B. Level of Risk
    C. Complementing or Replacing Base Pay
    D. Performance Criteria
    E. Time Horizon: Short-term versus Long-term

VI. Linking Incentive Pay with Competitive Strategy

Key Terms

Behavior encouragement plans are individual incentive pay plans that reward employees for specific behavioral accomplishments, such as good attendance or safety records. (p. 97)

Buy-back provision is a provision of the "Improshare" plan that rewards employee productivity up to a maximum level. Once that level is achieved, the rewards are set aside and accumulated for a one-time payout. If the maximum is achieved too often, the level is adjusted upward. (p. 105)

Company stock shares represent equity segments of stock whose equity interest increases positively with the number of stock shares. (p. 109)

Companywide incentive plans reward employees when the company exceeds minimum acceptable performance standards. (p. 106)

Deferred compensation rewards executives for meeting or exceeding performance standards with compensation that cannot be accessed until later. (p. 110)

Deferred profit sharing plans place cash awards in trust accounts for employees. These trusts are set aside on employees' behalf as a source of retirement income. (p. 107)

Employee stock option plans allow employees to purchase stock in their company. (p. 109)

ESOP (employee stock ownership plan) places company stock in trust accounts for employees. (p. 110)

Free rider effect refers to the employees who get an equal share of a group/team incentive reward even though their contributions were not as much as the other team members. (p. 106)

Gain sharing describes group incentive systems that provide participating employees an incentive payment based on improved company performance whether it be for increased productivity, increased customer satisfaction, lower costs, or better safety records. (p. 18)

Group incentive programs reward employees for their collective performance, rather than for each employee's individual performance. (p. 100)

Improshare is a specific kind of gain-sharing program that awards employees based on a labor hour ratio formula. A standard is determined by analyzing historical accounting data to find a relationship between the number of labor hours needed to complete a product. Productivity is then measured as a ratio of standard labor hours and actual labor hours. (p. 105)

Individual incentive plans reward employees for meeting work-related performance standards such as quality, productivity, customer satisfaction, safety, or attendance. Any one or combination of these standards may be used. (p. 96)

Labor hour ratio formula is part of the Improshare plan that rewards employees based on a standard that sets productivity levels by determining how many hours it took, in the past, to produce the same goods or service. (p. 105)

Management incentive plans award bonuses to managers when they meet or exceed objectives based on sales, profit, production, or other measures for their division, department, or unit. (p. 97)

Piecework plan is an individual incentive plan that is generally found in manufacturing settings and ties rewards to the amount of goods produced. (p. 96)

Profit-sharing plans pay a portion of company profits to employees, separate from base pay, cost-of-living adjustments, or permanent merit pay increases. Two basic kinds of profit-sharing plans are used widely today—current profit sharing and deferred profit sharing. (p. 107)

Referral plans are individual incentive pay plans that reward employees for referring new customers or recruiting successful job applicants. (p. 99)

Rucker Plan is a particular type of gain-sharing program that emphasizes employee involvement, and gain-sharing awards are based on the ratio between value added (less the costs of materials, supplies, and services rendered) and the total cost of employment. (p.103)

Scanlon Plan is a specific type of gain-sharing program that emphasizes employee involvement, and gain-sharing awards are based on the ratio between labor costs and sales value of production. (p. 103)

Team-based incentive plans (small-group incentive plans) reward team members after they meet specific objectives. (p. 100)

Value-added formula is part of the Rucker Plan that measures employee productivity by determining how much of the cost of a product is tied to the employee's contribution to the production of the product. (p. 103)

CHAPTER 5 REVIEW

Fill in the Blanks

Fill in the blanks with the appropriate terms.

A. Referral
B. Behavior encouragement
C. Lowest-cost
D. Deferred
E. Labor costs
F. Piecework
G. Group
H. Employee involvement systems
I. Improshare
J. Incentive pay
K. Gain sharing
L. Employee stock ownership plans
M. Equal incentive payment
N. Level of risk
O. Profit sharing

1. In the _____ competitive strategy, incentive pay is based on reducing the output costs per employee.

2. Receiving incentive pay for recruiting new employees is an example of the _____ incentive plan.

3. _____ is the most broadly used companywide incentive plan.

4. The _____ incentive plan is based on rewarding employees for meeting predetermined production goals.

5. Most gain-sharing incentive plans include a leadership philosophy, _____, and a bonus incentive.

6. The Scanlon Plan formula calls for dividing _____ by the sales value of production.

7. _____ incentive programs reward employees for their collective performance.

8. _____ is a specific gain-sharing program that awards employees based on a labor hour ration formula.

9. Two companywide incentive plans are profit sharing and _____.

10. In the _____ incentive plan, a group of employees is rewarded for increases in production.

11. In the _____ profit-sharing plan, the incentive pay is placed in trust accounts for employees.

12. The _____ incentive plan rewards employees for good attendance and good safety records.

13. _____ pay is compensation, other than base pay, earned by employees for meeting predetermined goals.

14. When designing incentive pay programs, the _____ chosen should depend on the extent to which employees control the attainment of the desired goals.

15. _____ approach rewards each team member the same regardless of their contribution to achieving the team's goal.

Multiple-Choice Questions

Circle the correct answer for each question.

1. In the differentiation competition strategy, *team-based incentives* and which other incentive plan are most appropriate?
   A. Individual
   B. Gain sharing
   C. Piecework
   D. Companywide

2. Which of the following is not considered an individual incentive program?
   A. Behavior encouragement plan
   B. Management incentive plan
   C. Piecework plan
   D. Gain-sharing plan

3. In this profit-sharing formula, employees share in company profits only when those profits fall between fixed minimum and maximum levels.
   A. Graduated first-dollar-of-profits
   B. Profitability threshold
   C. Standard percentage-of-profits
   D. Fixed first-dollar-of-profits

4. On which of the following assumptions is incentive pay **not** based?
   A. Employees differ in how much they can do and how well they can do it.
   B. A company's bottom line depends, in large part, on the productivity of its employees.
   C. Offering incentive pay is mandated by law.
   D. Rewarding employees for individual performances helps in hiring and keeping productive employees.

5. Which of the following is **not** considered an appropriate condition under which an individual incentive plan will work?
   A. Employees' performance cannot be measured objectively.
   B. Employees' performance can be measured objectively.
   C. Employees have sufficient control over work outcomes.
   D. The plan does not create fierce competition between employees.

6. Which of the following is a fundamental competitive strategy?
   A. Differentiation
   B. Highest productivity
   C. Lowest turnover
   D. Highest-cost

7. Which of the following is **not** considered an advantage of the individual incentive plan?
   A. It can enhance the relationship between pay and performance.
   B. It can promote equitable distribution of compensation.
   C. It is compatible with the work culture in the United States.
   D. It increases competition between employees.

8. If companies replace annual merit or seniority pay increases with fixed salaries and an incentive plan, how should it affect their payroll costs?
   A. Increase it
   B. Decrease it
   C. Control it
   D. Not affect it

9. Which of the following is **not** considered a disadvantage of the individual incentive plan?
   A. It can promote inflexibility in goal setting.
   B. Comprehensive performance measures are difficult to develop and maintain when improved work methods are implemented.
   C. It encourages undesirable workplace behaviors.
   D. Employees are forced to reach goals to receive the incentive pay.

10. Which of the following is **not** one of the general categories that most incentive pay plans are classified by?
    A. Group plans
    B. Individual plans
    C. Paired-team plans
    D. Companywide plans

11. The terms *buy-back provisions* and *labor hour ratio* are used in which gain-sharing plan formula:
    A. Scanlon Plan
    B. Fien Ratio Plan
    C. Improshare Plan
    D. Rucker Plan

12. In this profit-sharing formula, as the company's profits increase so does the employees' percentage of those profits.
    A. Graduated first-dollar-of-profits
    B. Profitability threshold
    C. Standard percentage-of-profits
    D. Fixed first-dollar-of-profits

13. Bonuses that are determined by dividing the total of (value added) − (costs of materials, supplies, and services rendered) by the (total employment costs) is the formula used in which gain-sharing plan?
    A. Scanlon Plan
    B. Fien Ratio Plan
    C. Improshare Plan
    D. Rucker Plan

14. In this profit-sharing formula, a specific percentage of the company's profits is given to employees when certain goals are met.
    A. Graduated first-dollar-of-profits
    B. Profitability threshold
    C. Standard percentage-of-profits
    D. Fixed first-dollar-of-profits

15. Bonuses that are determined by dividing (labor costs) by (the sum of revenue) + (the value of goods in inventory) is the formula used in which of the following gain-sharing plans:
    A. Scanlon Plan
    B. Fien Ratio Plan
    C. Improshare Plan
    D. Rucker Plan

Computer Exercise 5

Determining Current Profit Sharing Payouts

Currently Pizza Joe's has a profit sharing plan which covers all non-executive employees. Currently the pool is distributed evenly among all employees, but top management is concerned that mid-level managers who are making the most contribution to profits are receiving insufficient incentives. They want to shift to proportional payments based on each employee's salary, but do not wish to reduce the actual dollar amount of any employee's award. Luckily, they expect profits to significantly rise over each of the next 3 years. This year's pretax profits are projected to be 12 million dollars and 5% will be used to fund the profit sharing plan ($600,000). There are currently 2,000 employees. The lowest paid employees, entry Pizza Makers, make $7.50 per hour ($15,600 per year) and the average salary for mid-level managers is $75,000 per year.

Questions

Use the computer calculator to answer theses questions, record your answers on the Answer Sheets. Print your answers when the exercise is completed. To simplify this exercise assume that base salaries are not increasing during the periods in question and the profits projected for this year are accurate.

1. Answer the following questions to determine the size of the bonus the average mid-level manager would receive if she is awarded the same percentage of salary as that paid to the Pizza Makers.
   A. What is this year's total profit sharing pool and each employee's bonus (pool / 2,000)? 300
   B. The entry Pizza Makers' bonuses will equal what percent of their base pay (bonus / 15,600 X 100)? 1.9%
   C. What size bonus would the average mid-level manager receive if she is awarded the same percentage of salary as that paid to the Pizza Makers (75,000 X percent in 1B)? 1425

2. Assuming a payroll of $60 million per year, what size profit sharing pool is required to ensure that all employees receive a bonus equal to 2% of their earnings (payroll X .02)? 1.2 MILLION

3. What percentage of profits must Pizza Joe's pay to fund the profit sharing pool calculated in question 2, assuming they earn the profits below? Divide the pool from question 2 by the profits below and multiply by 100:
   A. 12 million 10%
   B. 15 million 8%
   C. 18 million 6.7%
   D. 24 million 5%

4. Pizza Joe's decides to allocate 7% of profits to the profit sharing pool and to distribute the pool based on equal proportions (percents) of employee's annual salary. They have a 60 million dollar payroll and 18 million in profits.
    A. What is the size of the profit sharing pool (18,000,000 X .07)? 1.26 million
    B. What percent of salary will each employee receive (pool / 60,000,000 X 100)? 2.1%
    C. How much is the Pizza Makers' bonus? (Divide the percent in 4B by 100 and multiply by the annual salary.) $327.60
    D. How much is the average Mid-level Managers' bonus? $1575

Further Study

Write your response to these questions on the appropriate Answer Sheet.

F1. Assuming that first year awards are paid based on the results of question 4 above, how do you think the Pizza Makers and Mid-level Managers will respond to the profit sharing plan during its second year? Do you think this incentive plan will increase profits? YES
IT'S NOT GOING TO HURT ANYTHING.

F2. Assume that under this plan profits increase steadily for three years, but then Pizza Joe's experiences a loss due to new competition. How do you think the Pizza Makers and Middle Managers will respond to this plan following the loss? Do you think that this incentive plan will help Pizza Joe's become profitable again?
EMPLOYEES WILL BE UPSET

CHAPTER 6
Person-Focused Pay

Learning Objectives

1. Differing opinions about the meaning of competency-based pay
2. Traditional person-focused pay plans—pay-for-knowledge pay and skill-based pay programs
3. Reasons that companies adopt pay-for-knowledge and skill-based pay programs
4. Pay-for-knowledge plan and skill-based pay variations
5. Contrasts between person-focused pay systems and incentive (variable) pay or merit pay concepts
6. Advantages and disadvantages of using pay-for-knowledge plans and skill-based pay plans
7. How pay-for-knowledge plans and skill-based pay plans fit with differentiation and lowest cost competitive strategies

Chapter Outline

I. **Defining Competency-Based Pay, Pay-For-Knowledge, and Skill-Based Pay**

II. **Usage of Pay-for-Knowledge Pay Programs**

III. **Reasons to Adopt Pay-for-Knowledge Pay Programs**
   A. Technological Innovation
   B. Increased Global Competition

IV. **Varieties of Pay-for-Knowledge Pay Programs**

V. **Contrasting Person-Focused Pay with Job-Based Pay**

VI. **Advantages of Pay-for-Knowledge Pay Programs**
   A. Advantages to Employees
   B. Advantages to Employers

VII. **Disadvantages of Pay-for-Knowledge Pay Programs**

VIII. **Linking Pay-for-Knowledge Pay with Competitive Strategy**

Key Terms

Competency-based pay usually refers to "pay-for-knowledge" and "skill-based pay" programs, which awards employees for successfully acquiring new job-related knowledge or skills. (p. 118)

Cross-departmental models promote staffing flexibility by training employees in one department with some of the critical skills they would need to perform effectively in other departments (p. 126)

Depth of knowledge refers to the level of specialization, based on job-related knowledge, an employee brings to a particular job. (p. 120)

Depth of skills refers to the level of specialization, based on skills, an employee brings to a particular job. (p.120)

Horizontal knowledge refers to similar knowledge (i.e., record keeping applied to payroll applications and record keeping applied to employee benefits). (p. 120)

Horizontal skills refer to similar skills (i.e., assembly skills applied to lawn mowers and assembly skills applied to snowblowers). (p. 120)

Job-based pay compensates employees for jobs they currently perform. (p. 128)

Job-point accrual model is a type of pay-for-knowledge program that provides employees opportunities to develop skills and learn to perform jobs from different job families. (p. 126)

Pay-for-knowledge plans reward managerial, service, or professional workers for successfully learning specific curricula. (p. 118)

Skill-based pay, used mostly for employees who do physical work, increases these workers' pay as they master new skills. (p. 120)

Skill blocks model is a kind of pay-for-knowledge program that applies to jobs from within the same job family. Just as in the stair-step model (see below), employees progress to increasingly complex jobs. However, in a skill blocks program, skills do not necessarily build on each other. (p. 125)

Skill level-performance matrix is a type of pay-for-knowledge program that rewards employees according to how well they have applied skills and knowledge to their jobs. (p. 129)

Stair-step model is a type of pay-for-knowledge program that resembles a flight of stairs. The steps represent jobs from a particular job family that differ in terms of complexity. Skills at higher levels build upon previous lower-level skills. (p. 123)

Vertical knowledge refers to knowledge traditionally associated with supervisory activities (i.e., performance appraisal and grievance review procedures). (p. 120)

Vertical skills are those skills traditionally considered supervisory skills, such as scheduling, coordinating, training, and leading others. (p. 120)

CHAPTER 6 REVIEW

Fill in the Blanks

Fill in the blanks with the appropriate terms.

A. Vertical
B. Cross-departmental
C. Competitive advantages
D. Depth of skills
E. Entitlement
F. Skill-based pay
G. Global competition
H. Horizontal
I. Job-based pay
J. Job-point accrual
K. Pay-for-knowledge
L. Stair-step
M. Merit pay
N. Skill-level-performance matrix
O. Skill variety

1. As opposed to the skill blocks model, the _____ model addresses the development of knowledge or skills depth.

2. The job-point accrual model is similar to the _____ model.

3. _____ compensation plans reward employees for mastering new job skills.

4. In order to establish and maintain _____, companies should carefully consider adopting competency-based pay systems.

5. According to the job characteristics theory, employees will be more motivated to work if the job offers task identity, autonomy, _____, and feedback.

6. _____ compensation plans reward employees for successfully gaining specific new job-related knowledge.

7. _____ compensates employees depending on how well they fulfilled their work roles and met designated goals.

8. In the competency-based plan, _____ skills refer to the learning of new skills that are similar to the ones the employee already has.

9. _____ refers to the level of expertise an employee brings to a particular job.

10. Pay-for-knowledge programs imply that employees must move away from viewing pay as a/an _____.

11. One of the biggest reasons American companies must become more productive is _____.

12. In the _____ pay-for-knowledge model, employees are encouraged to develop skills and learn to perform jobs from different job families.

13. In the _____ model, employees are rewarded according to *how well* they have applied skills and knowledge to their jobs.

14. _____ compensates employees for the work they are currently doing.

15. In the competency-based plan, _____ skills are traditionally considered supervisory skills.

Multiple-Choice Questions

Circle the correct answer for each question.

1. When properly designed and implemented, these programs can lead to enhanced job performance, reduced staffing, and greater flexibility.
   A. Job-based programs
   B. Pay-for-knowledge programs
   C. Diversity pay programs
   D. Competitive pay programs

2. In this pay-for-knowledge program, an employee's compensation amount increases as he or she learns new, more complex skills that build on a depth of knowledge within a specific job family.
   A. Job-point accrual model
   B. Stair-step model
   C. Interdepartmental model
   D. Skill blocks model

3. Which of the following is **not** a dimension of the competency-based pay plan?
   A. Vertical knowledge
   B. Vertical skills
   C. Lateral skills
   D. Depth of skills

4. This pay-for-knowledge program compensates employees for increasing their depth of skills or knowledge within a particular job family.
   A. Stair-step model
   B. Job-based model
   C. Skill-based model
   D. Job-point model

5. To insure that an employee applies the newly learned knowledge to a job, companies might want to combine which two compensation plans?

   A. Pay-for-knowledge and pay-for-performance
   B. Pay-for-knowledge and seniority pay
   C. Pay-for-knowledge and stock options
   D. Pay-for-knowledge and piecework

6. Which of the following is not considered a pay-for-knowledge program?

   A. Job-point accrual model
   B. Stair-step model
   C. Interdepartmental model
   D. Skill blocks model

7. According to the job characteristic theory, this core characteristic is defined as "the degree to which the job is important to others—both inside and outside the company."

   A. Skill variety
   B. Task identity
   C. Job status
   D. Autonomy

8. According to the job characteristic theory, this core characteristic is defined as "the degree to which the job or employer provides the employee with clear and direct information about job outcomes and performance."

   A. Feedback
   B. Two-way communication
   C. Job description
   D. Task identity

9. Competency-based pay is another name for which compensation program?

   A. Vertical skills pay
   B. Vertical knowledge pay
   C. Horizontal skills pay
   D. Pay-for-knowledge

10. In this pay-for-knowledge program, an employee's compensation amount increases as he or she learns new, more complex skills that do **not** necessarily build on each other.

    A. Job-point accrual model
    B. Stair-step model
    C. Interdepartmental model
    D. Skill blocks model

11. This term is used to describe the compensation practice that pays employees who have performed the assigned duties of their position and have met predetermined production goals.

    A. Job-based pay
    B. Pay-for-knowledge
    C. Merit pay
    D. Skill-based pay

12. In this pay-for-knowledge program, employees are encouraged to acquire new skills and knowledge in areas outside their job family, in order to promote staffing flexibility.

    A. Job-point accrual model
    B. Skill blocks model
    C. Cross-departmental model
    D. Stair-step model

13. This term is used when referring to the amount of skills an employee has in performing the duties of a particular job.

    A. Job-based skills
    B. Vertical skills
    C. Job-point skills
    D. Depth of skills

14. Which of the following is **not** one of the three advantages the pay-for-knowledge system provides to employees?

    A. Enhanced job performance
    B. Lower hourly labor costs
    C. Reduced staffing
    D. Greater flexibility

15. In this pay-for-knowledge program, employees are encouraged to develop both their vertical and horizontal skills within a particular job family.

    A. Stair-step model
    B. Skill blocks model
    C. Job-point accrual model
    D. Skill-based model

Computer Exercise 6

Implementing a Pay-for-Knowledge Program

Pizza Joe's is opening a new plant and plans to use a stair-step pay plan for the clerical positions. There will be 5 steps in the plan and each will have the following core requirements: proficient in filing, typing (45 words per minute minimum speed), and one word processing program. In addition, employees must demonstrate proficiency, complete the appropriate courses at a community college, or complete the appropriate Pizza Joe's training (at Pizza Joe's University!) prior to moving to the next step in the program. The core electives and monthly rates of pay are as follows:

Clerk I - $1,320
1. Entry, core requirements

Clerk II - $1,424
1. Maintaining office supplies inventory
2. Ordering office supplies from local vendor

Clerk III - $1,528
1. Core electives for Clerk II
2. Proficient in one spreadsheet program e.g., Excel or Lotus 1-2-3.
3. Proficient in one additional word processing program.

Clerk IV - $1,632
1. Core electives for Clerk III
2. Accounts receivable ledgers
3. Accounts payable ledgers

Clerk V - $1,736
1. Core electives for Clerk IV
2. Maintaining payroll records
3. Supervisory skills

Initially the program will not include optional electives. The Director of Compensation has asked you to project direct payroll costs and the distribution of clerks across different steps over time. She has told you to assume that the following clerks will be hired: 5 Clerk I's, 4 Clerk II's, and 1 Clerk III.

Questions

Each question below makes assumptions about the frequency and rate of movement from one step (I, II, III, etc.) to another. Move the people on the computer chart as directed by the question. At the end of the period in question, count how many employees are at each step. Move the highest paid clerks first. Assume that all promotions are effective at the last day of a period, e.g. end of a 6 month period, end of one year, etc. To calculate the total monthly payroll, multiply the number of clerks at each step by the monthly rate of pay for that step and sum the payroll for each step. (All payroll figures are given in today's dollars so they can be compared across time. In reality the pay structure would be increased over time, but this would presumably reflect the same purchasing power.)

1. Assume that 1 clerk at each step moves to the next step every 6 months.
    A. How many clerks are at each step and what is the monthly payroll at the end of 1 year?
    B. How many clerks are at each step and what is the monthly payroll at the end of 2 years?

2. Answer all the same questions as question 1, but assume that 2 clerks at each step move up every 6 months.

3. Assume that 2 clerks at each step move to the next step each **year**, that one of the highest paid clerks resigns each year, and that you simultaneously hire a new Clerk. (Move the highest paid computer person to the lowest step to simulate the resignation and new hire.)
    A. How many clerks are at each step and what is the monthly payroll at the end of 1 year ?
    B. How many clerks are at each step and what is the monthly payroll at the end of 2 years ?

Further Study

F1. Develop your own assumptions regarding the rate of movement and turnover of clerks.
    A. List your assumptions.
    B. How many clerks are at each step and what is the monthly payroll at the end of 1 year ?
    C. How many clerks are at each step and what is the monthly payroll at the end of 2 years?

CHAPTER 7
Building Internally Consistent Compensation Systems

Learning Objectives

1. The importance of building internally consistent compensation systems
2. The process of job analysis
3. Job descriptions
4. O*NET
5. The process of job evaluation
6. A variety of job evaluation techniques
7. Alternatives to job evaluation
8. Internally consistent compensation systems and competitive strategy

Chapter Outline

I. Job Analysis
   A. Steps in the Job Analysis Process
   B. Legal Considerations for Job Analysis
   C. Job Analysis Techniques
   D. U.S. Department of Labor (DOL) Occupational Information Network (O*NET)

II. Job Evaluation
   A. Compensable Factors
   B. The Job Evaluation Process

III. Job Evaluation Techniques
   A. The Point Method
   B. Alternative Job Content Evaluation Approaches
   C. Alternatives to Job Evaluation

IV. Internally Consistent Compensation Systems and Competitive Strategy

Key Terms

Ability, based on Equal Employment Opportunity Commission guidelines, refers to a present competence to perform an observable behavior or a behavior that results in an observable product. (p. 147)

Alternation ranking is a job ranking method where committee members judge the relative value of jobs according to a single criterion such as job complexity or the centrality of the job to the company's competitive strategy. (p. 166)

Basic skills refer to information that describes developed capacities that facilitate learning or the more rapid acquisition of knowledge. (p. 150)

Benchmark jobs provide reference points against which jobs within a company are judged. (p. 162)

Classification plans place jobs into categories based on compensable factors. (p. 166)

Compensable factors are the salient job characteristics by which companies establish relative pay rates. (p. 159)

Experience and training refers to the specific preparation required for entry into a job and past work experience contributing to qualifications for an occupation. (p. 148)

Generalized work activities refers to the general types of job behaviors occurring on multiple jobs. (p. 150)

Interests refer to worker characteristics that describe the worker's preferences for work environments and outcomes. (p. 150)

Internally consistent compensation systems clearly define the relative value of each job among all jobs within a company. (p. 138)

Job analysis is a systematic process for gathering, documenting, and analyzing information in order to describe jobs. (p. 140)

Job content refers to the actual activities that employees must perform on the job. Job content descriptions may be broad, general statements of job activities or detailed descriptions of duties and tasks performed in the job. (p. 140)

Job-content evaluation, an approach to job evaluation, emphasizes the company's internal value system, establishing a hierarchy of internal job worth based on each job's role in company strategy. (p. 161)

Job descriptions summarize a job's purpose and list its tasks, duties, and responsibilities, as well as the skills, knowledge, and abilities necessary to perform the job at a minimum level. (p. 145)

Job evaluations are tasks that help to systematically recognize differences in the relative worth among a set of jobs and establish pay differentials. (p. 159)

Job summary, a statement contained in job descriptions, summarizes the job based on two to four descriptive statements. (p. 145)

Knowledge, based on Equal Employment Opportunity Commission guidelines, refers to a body of information applied directly to the performance of a function. (p. 147)

Market-based evaluations use market data to determine differences in job worth. (p. 161)

Occupational characteristics refer to information that describes labor market information, occupational outlook, and wages. (p. 150)

Occupational Information Network (O*NET) is a database designed to describe jobs in the relatively new service sector of the economy, and to more accurately describe jobs that evolved as the result of technological advances. O*NET replaces the *Revised Handbook for Analyzing Jobs*. (p. 150)

Organizational context refers to information that indicates the characteristics of the organization that influence the nature of work. (p. 150)

Paired comparison is a job-ranking technique that compares the value of every job in a company to every other job, with the position that wins most of the comparisons being the highest-ranked position. (p. 166)

Point method is a job-content valuation technique that uses quantitative methodology. (p. 161)

Reliable job analysis yields consistent results under similar conditions. (p. 144)

Simple ranking plans order all jobs from lowest to highest according to a single criterion such as job complexity or the centrality of the job to the company's competitive strategy. (p. 165)

Skill, based on Equal Employment Opportunity Commission guidelines, refers to an observable competence to perform a learned psychomotor act. (p. 147)

Universal compensable factors refer to the four factors (skill, effort, responsibility, and working conditions) that are common in most jobs. (p. 159)

Valid job analysis method accurately assesses each job's duties. (p. 144)

Worker characteristics refer to information that includes a worker's abilities, interests, and work styles. (p. 150)

Worker specification, a section in job descriptions, lists the education, skills, abilities, knowledge, and other qualifications individuals must possess to perform the job adequately. (p. 147)

Work styles refer to the personal characteristics that describe important interpersonal and work style requirements in jobs and occupations. (p. 150)

CHAPTER 7 REVIEW

Fill in the Blanks

Fill in the blanks with the appropriate terms.

A. Reliable job analysis
B. Job description
C. Job analysis
D. Worker requirements
E. Job evaluation
F. Job content
G. Benchmark jobs
H. Simple ranking plan
I. Internally consistent job structures
J. Point method
K. Job summary
L. Valid job analysis
M. Compensable factors
N. Market-based evaluation
O. Internally consistent compensation systems

1. _____ are salient job characteristics that companies use in their job evaluations to establish relative pay rates

2. _____ is a systematic process for gathering, documenting, and analyzing information in order to describe jobs.

3. The _____ clearly define the relative value of each job among all the jobs within a company.

4. A/An _____ systematically recognizes differences in the relative worth management places among a set of jobs to establish pay differences.

5. _____ are used in job evaluations to develop factors, and they represent the entire range of jobs in a company.

6. _____ summarizes a job's purpose and lists its tasks, duties, and responsibilities, as well as the skills, knowledge, and abilities necessary to perform the job at a minimum level.

7. A _____ is conducted when two job analysts independently observe an employee's job performance and come to the same conclusion.

8. _____ are the minimum qualifications employees must have to perform a job.

9. _____ describes job duties and tasks as well as pertinent factors such as skill and effort (compensable factors) needed to perform the job adequately.

10. _____ is a job-content valuation technique that uses quantitative methodology to determine the relative worth of jobs.

11. Conducting a _____ requires getting job-related data from multiple sources and using multiple methods to gather the information.

12. _____ is a brief, concise description of a job that usually states whether the employee has a supervisor, and if so, who that person is.

13. The _____ job evaluation method orders all jobs from lowest to highest according to a single criterion such as job complexity or the centrality of the job to the company's competitive strategy.

14. _____ is a job evaluation method that is used when a company wants to assign job pay rates that are comparable to the rates other companies pay for similar positions.

15. The _____ formally recognize differences in job characteristics, and thereby enable compensation managers to set pay accordingly.

Multiple-Choice Questions

Circle the correct answer for each question.

1. This job evaluation plan emphasizes a company's internal value system to establish a hierarchy of internal job worth based on each job's role in company strategy.
   A. Market-based
   B. Market-content
   C. Job-based
   D. Job-content

2. When using the point method job evaluation technique, the maximum point value for each compensable factor is determined by multiplying each factor by how much?
   A. The sales volume of the competition
   B. 150
   C. The number of points decided by the company's compensation professional
   D. 100

3. Internally consistent job structures are created using job analysis and which other process?
   A. Job evaluation
   B. Job content
   C. Job summaries
   D. Classification plans

4. Once a benchmark job has been selected and the compensable factors have been determined, the next three steps (in order), in the point method evaluation technique are
   A. determine the factors' point values, define the factors' weights, and define factors' degrees.
   B. define the factors' weights, determine the factors' point values, and define factors' degrees.
   C. define factors' degrees, define the factors' weights, and determine the factors' point values.
   D. define factors' degrees, determine the factors' point values, and define the factors' weights.

5. Two common variations of the simple ranking plan are the alternation ranking plan and which other?
   A. Paired comparison
   B. Job summary
   C. Point method
   D. Job descriptions

6. This book contains a comprehensive list of over 20,000 job descriptions.
   A. *Encyclopedia of Occupations*
   B. *Dictionary of Job Titles*
   C. *Encyclopedia of Job Titles*
   D. *Dictionary of Occupational Titles*

7. According to the EEOC, this term refers to a body of information that can be applied directly to the performance of a job function.
   A. Skill
   B. Ability
   C. Knowledge
   D. Technique

8. This section of a job description describes the major activities and, if pertinent, the supervisory responsibilities.
   A. Job title
   B. Job summary
   C. Job duties
   D. Worker specifications

9. This word is used to describe the systematic process for gathering, documenting, and analyzing information in order to describe jobs.
    A. Job analysis
    B. Job evaluation
    C. Job content
    D. Job summary

10. This section of a job description lists the education, skills, abilities, knowledge, and other qualifications employees must have to perform the job adequately.
    A. Job title
    B. Job summary
    C. Job duties
    D. Worker specifications

11. This word is used to describe the smallest step into which any work activity may be subdivided.
    A. Task
    B. Position
    C. Occupation
    D. Element

12. According to the EEOC, this term refers to a present competence to perform an observable behavior that results in an observable product.
    A. Skill
    B. Ability
    C. Knowledge
    D. Technique

13. A collection of steps necessary to perform the duties of a total work assignment is called a
    A. task.
    B. element.
    C. position.
    D. occupation.

14. This job evaluation plan uses data from other companies to determine differences in job worth.
    A. Market-based
    B. Market-content
    C. Job-based
    D. Job-content

15. Human resource activities designed to determine descriptions are part of which of the following processes?
    A. Job content
    B. Job analysis
    C. Worker requirement designation
    D. Job structure

Computer Exercise 7

Conducting a Job Evaluation

The Director of Compensation has asked you to re-evaluate a Human Resource Manager I position for the South Bend, Indiana Plant. The Plant Manager wants to promote the incumbent to Human Resource Manager II. The Director gives you the memo below which she says is accurate.

To: Director of Compensation

From: Plant Manager, South Bend, Indiana

Subject: H.R. Manager Promotion

I request that our H.R. Manager position be re-evaluated and changed from a H.R. Manager I to a H.R. Manager II and that the incumbent be immediately promoted. I realize that H.R. Manager II positions have previously only been approved in plants with over 350 employees, but I feel strongly that the size of the plant should not be the only variable considered. Please consider the following during your review:

1. We are growing faster than any other plant at Pizza Joe's. This places stress on all our H.R. programs. In addition, I personally rely heavily on the H.R. Manager to design, implement, and evaluate new H.R. programs which will help our plant and the company as a whole.

2. Although Ms. Lewis was only hired 14 months ago as our H.R. Manager, she has already implemented a new temporary agency program which is expected to save the plant $250,000. She has also implemented a job-sharing program which has improved productivity and helped retain two of our most talented employees. Other Plant H.R. Managers and company H.R. Specialists have sought her advice about both programs, as well as other areas of her expertise.

3. Ms. Lewis meets the qualifications for H.R. Manager II including: a B.A. in Human Resources and 10 years of progressively responsible H.R. experience, including expertise in contingent employment, compensation, employee relations, and EEO.

The revised job description is enclosed for your review. Please call Ms. Lewis or I if you have any questions. I look forward to your speedy response since I do not know how long we can keep such a talented person at this salary level.

S.A. Miller

You are also given current job descriptions for H.R. Manager I and II, the points assigned to those jobs, and Pizza Joe's Point Method Job Evaluation System.

Current Job Descriptions

Human Resource Manager I

Incumbent is responsible for managing the overall human resource program for a small plant (generally fewer than 250 employees). The position reports directly to the Plant Manager, but receives guidance from the Human Resource Department. Duties typically include:

1. Reviews company H.R. policies and programs and advises the Plant Manager regarding local implementation. Administers local benefit, payroll, and personnel records program; supervises assistant; and counsels employees concerning H.R. policies and procedures.

2. Advises plant management on the full range of H.R. practices and procedures including recruitment, placement, training, employee relations, and EEO. Reviews and resolves sensitive issues. Seeks assistance as needed from company H.R. specialists.

3. May analyze and conduct a broad range of studies as needed, reports findings to the Plant Manager and/or the HR Department.

Job evaluation points:

Skill	degree 2	240 points
Responsibility	degree 2	100 points
Effort	degree 2	40 points
Working Conditions	degree 2	20 points
Total		**400 points**

Human Resource Manager II

Incumbent is responsible for independently managing the overall human resource program for a large complex plant (generally more than 350 employees). She/he is responsible for supervising management and non-management employees. The incumbent reports directly to the Plant Manager and collaborates with the Human Resource Department to discuss alternative approaches and recommend changes in company policy. H.R. employees outside the plant may seek incumbent's advice in incumbent's area of expertise. Duties typically include:

1. Reviews and analyzes company H.R. policies and programs and applicable federal and state laws, develops or adapts HR programs to meet the plant's needs, and works with the Plant Manager to implement local programs and policies.

2. Provides direction to and supervises staff of one or more H.R. Specialists and H.R. Assistants. Oversees or administers: local benefit, payroll, and personnel records programs; contracts with local employment agencies or contractors; and the employee counseling program.

3. Advises plant management on the full range of H.R. practices and procedures including recruitment, placement, training, employee relations, discipline, discharge, and EEO. Reviews and resolves sensitive issues. Coordinates with company H.R. specialists and keeps them informed of sensitive issues e.g. discharges, EEO complaints, etc.

4. Determines the need for, supervises, and participates as needed in the development and maintenance of H.R. programs, systems, and studies to increase H.R. effectiveness. Studies may include: organizational reviews; salary surveys and other pay related studies; recruitment, testing, and placement studies; training effectiveness, etc. Makes recommendations to the Plant Manager on how to improve plant management and recommends changes as need to company H.R. programs and policies.

Job evaluation points:

Skill	degree 3	360 points
Responsibility	degree 3	150 points
Effort	degree 3	60 points
Working Conditions	degree 2	20 points
Total		**590 points**

Revised Job Description

Human Resource Manager (level to be determined from job evaluation)
South Bend, Indiana

Incumbent is responsible for independently managing the overall human resource program for a dynamic, growing, complex plant (225 regular employees, 4 part-time regular employees, 20 temporary employees, and intermittent contractors). The position significantly impacts plant operations and improves H.R. management throughout the company. The incumbent reports directly to the Plant Manager and collaborates with the

Human Resource Department to discuss alternative approaches and recommend changes in company policy. H.R. employees outside the plant regularly seek her advice. Duties typically include:

1. Reviews and analyzes company H.R. policies and programs and applicable federal and state laws, develops or adapts HR programs to meet the plant's needs, and works with the Plant Manager to implement local programs and policies.

2. Provides direction to and supervises staff of two part-time regular H.R. Assistants. Oversees or administers: local benefit, payroll, and personnel records programs; contracts with local employment agencies or contractors; and the employee counseling program.

3. Advises plant management on the full range of H.R. practices and procedures including recruitment, placement, training, employee relations, discipline, discharge, and EEO. Reviews and resolves sensitive issues. Coordinates with company H.R. specialists and keeps them informed of sensitive issues e.g. discharges, EEO complaints, etc.

4. Determines the need for, supervises, and participates as needed in the development and maintenance of H.R. programs, systems, and studies to increase H.R. effectiveness. Studies may include: organizational reviews; salary surveys and other pay related studies; recruitment, testing, and placement studies; training effectiveness, etc. Makes recommendations to the Plant Manager on how to improve plant management and recommends changes as need to company H.R. programs and policies.

Pizza Joe's Point Method Job Evaluation System

Compensable Factors	Degree 1	Degree 2	Degree 3	Degree 4	Degree 5
Skill	120	240	360	480	600
Responsibility	50	100	150	200	250
Effort	20	40	60	80	100
Working Conditions	10	20	30	40	50

The degree definitions for the compensable factors are listed below. To simplify the exercise definitions are only given for pertinent degrees.

Compensable Factors	Degree	Definition
Skill	2	Requires application of principles and procedures to moderately complex problems which impact on the local work group. Requires a BA/BS and 1-3 years experience.
	3	Requires application of principles and procedures to complex problems which significantly impact the local work group and/or moderately impact the company. Requires a BA/BS and 4-7 years experience.
Responsibility	2	Sets priorities, uses independent judgment and discretion to solve moderately complex problems while under general supervision. May supervise non-management employees.
	3	Supervises a staff of management and non-management employees, sets priorities for the work group, uses independent judgment and discretion to initiate new programs or solve complex problems. Works under broad supervision
Effort	2	Position requires physical effort typical of an office environment. Incumbent must work diligently to produce high quality work within deadlines.
	3	In addition to above, incumbent initiates new programs and/or must maintain expertise in his/her field.
Working Conditions	2	Generally works in an office with minimal physical hazards. Spends time in plants to supervise or meet with employees.

Point Conversion: **Human Resource Manager I - 390 to 470 points**
    Human Resource Manager II - 480 to 600 points

Questions

Familiarize yourself with the job evaluation system and degree definitions for each compensable factor by reviewing the degrees and points assigned to the current H.R. Manager I and II jobs. Compare the revised job description with the other two descriptions and with the degree definitions for each compensable factor. Enter your answers and print when the exercise is completed.

1. Evaluate the revised position by assigning the appropriate points for each compensable factor. Assume that the position must **fully** meet the degree definition prior to receiving points for that degree. Record your evaluation in the chart in computer exercise 7 (i.e., click on your chosen point totals for each compensable factor) and the computer will sum the points you have assigned to the job. Compare the total points with the point conversion guide and enter the proper title.

2. Evaluate the position again, but choose the degree definition that **best** fits the job even if the position does not fully meet the definition. Record your evaluation in the chart in computer exercise 7 (i.e., click on your chosen point totals for each compensable factor) and the computer will sum the points you have assigned to the job. Compare the total points with the point conversion guide and enter the proper title.

3. Based on your personal judgment, do you believe that this position should be evaluated as a H.R. Manager I or II? Explain your reasoning on the Answer Sheet.

Further Study

F1. Currently, the compensable factors are weighted as follows: Skill - 60% of the points, Responsibility - 25% of the points, Effort 10 % of the points, and Working Conditions 5% of the points. Assume that Pizza Joe's decides to change the weighting so that the weights for Skill and Responsibility are now reversed (see chart). Re-evaluate the position based on the new weights. Assume that the position must **fully** meet the degree definition prior to receiving points for that degree. Record your evaluation in the chart, compare the total points with the point conversion guide and enter the proper title on the Answer Sheet.

CHAPTER 8

Building Market-Competitive Compensation Systems

Learning Objectives

1. Market-competitive compensation systems
2. Compensation surveys
3. Statistical analysis of compensation surveys
4. Integrating the internal job structure with external market pay rates
5. Compensation policies and strategic mandates

Chapter Outline

I. **Market-Competitive Pay Systems: The Basic Building Blocks**

II. **Compensation Surveys**

    A. Preliminary Considerations

    B. Using Published Compensation Survey Data

    C. Compensation Surveys: Strategic Considerations

    D. Compensation Survey Data

III. **Integrating Internal Job Structures with External Market Pay Rates**

IV. **Compensation Policies and Strategic Mandates**

Key Terms

Central tendency represents the fact that a set of data cluster or center around a central point. Central tendency is a number that represents the typical numerical value in a data set. (p. 182)

Comparable worth represents an ongoing debate in society regarding pay differentials between men and women who perform similar, but not identical work. (p. 190)

Compensation surveys involve the collection and subsequent analysis of competitors' compensation data. (p. 172)

Market lag policy distinguishes companies from the competition by compensating employees less than most competitors. (p. 192)

Market lead policy distinguishes companies from the competition by compensating employees more highly that most competitors. (p. 192)

Market match policy most closely follows the typical market pay rates because companies pay according to the market pay line. Thus, pay rates fall along the market pay line. (p. 192)

Market pay line is used in regression analysis as a representative of typical market pay rates relative to a company's job structure. (p. 189)

Mean is a method of determining an average amount (i.e., salary) by adding all the amounts together and dividing that total by the number of amounts used. (p. 182)

Median is a method of determining a middle value in an ordered sequence of numerical data. (p. 183)

Occupational classification refers to a group of two or more jobs that are based on similar work characteristics and responsibilities. (p. 177)

Percentiles describe dispersion by indicating the percentage of figures that fall below certain points. There are 100 percentiles ranging from the first percentile to the 100th percentile. (p. 185)

Quartiles describe dispersion by indicating the percentage of figures that fall below certain points. There are four quartiles. (p. 185)

Regression analysis is a statistical analysis technique used to allow compensation professionals to establish pay rates that are consistent with typical pay rates for jobs in external markets. (p. 189)

Relevant labor markets represent the fields of potentially qualified candidates for particular jobs. (p. 176)

Standard deviation refers to the mean distance of each salary figure from the mean. (p. 184)

Variation represents the amount of spread or dispersion in a set of data. (p. 184)

CHAPTER 8 REVIEW

Fill in the Blanks

Fill in the blanks with the appropriate term.

A. Relevant labor markets
B. Benchmark jobs
C. Variation
D. Central tendency
E. External market factors
F. Occupational classification
G. Compensation surveys
H. Median
I. Internal factors
J. Market pay line
K. Standard deviation
L. Mean
M. Market lead policy
N. Comparable worth
O. Labor market assessments

1. A company that decides to pay their new employees less that than their competitors is probably following a(n) _____.

2. The _____ represents the typical market pay rates relative to a company's job structure.

3. _____ are used as reference points for setting pay levels.

4. In a strategic analysis, industry profiles, information about competitors, and long-term growth prospects are examples of a company's _____

5. _____ refers to a group of two or more jobs that are based on similar work characteristics, duties, and responsibilities.

6. _____ represents the amount of spread or dispersion in a set of data.

7. _____ are done to determine the availability of qualified employees.

8. _____ is a number that represents the typical numerical value in a data set

9. _____ enable companies to make sound judgments about how much to pay employees.

10. In statistics, the _____ of employees' salaries would be calculated by adding up all the salary amounts and dividing the total by the number of salaries.

11. In a strategic analysis, financial condition, marketing, and human resources are examples of a company's _____.

12. In statistics, _____ refers to the average distance each salary figure is from the mean.

13. When a company decides to pay their employees more than their competition, it means they are probably following a(n) _____.

14. In statistics, the _____ of employees' salaries would be determined by ranking the salaries and selecting the one in the middle.

15. _____ are defined on the basis of occupational classification, geography, and product or service market competitors.

Multiple-Choice Questions

Circle the correct answer for each question.

1. When calculating the mean of a salary data set, the mean will understate the "true" typical value when what occurs?
    A. All the salary figures are tightly bunched.
    B. There are one or more extremely large outliers.
    C. There are one or more extremely small outliers
    D. There are no outliers in the data set.

2. Which of the following is **not** a characteristic of benchmark jobs?
    A. The jobs are common across a number of different employers.
    B. The jobs are generally accepted in the labor market for the purposes of setting pay levels.
    C. The jobs represent the entire range of jobs that are being evaluated within a company.
    D. The jobs must be above the entry level position

3. Which of the following was **not** mentioned as a reason that companies do not develop their own compensation surveys?
    A. The surveys can be costly to develop.
    B. Many companies are hesitant to share compensation information.
    C. Company-made surveys are not as accurate
    D. Many companies do not have employees qualified to develop the surveys.

4. This pay level policy most closely follows the typical market pay rates because companies pay according to the market pay policy.
    A. Market match policy
    B. Market lag policy
    C. Market lead policy
    D. Market share policy

5. Quartiles and percentiles indicate the percentage of observations that relate in what way, to a certain point.
   A. Rise above it
   B. Are furthest from it
   C. Fall below it
   D. Match it

6. Which of the following is **not** considered a characteristic of compensation survey data?
   A. There is an immense amount of data on most surveys.
   B. Most of the data is not always as current companies would like them to be.
   C. Compensation professionals must use statistical analyses to integrate their internal job structures with the data.
   D. The data must be reliable and valid.

7. All but one of the following were listed in the book as internal capabilities that need to be examined in a strategic analysis.
   A. Available manpower
   B. Functional capabilities
   C. Financial condition
   D. Human resource capabilities

8. Which of the following is **not** a reason for a company to use an existing compensation survey?
   A. Most companies lack qualified employees to develop a survey.
   B. Custom surveys may be cheaper.
   C. Rival companies might be reluctant to provide information to a competitor.
   D. Custom surveys may be more costly.

9. This word is used to represent the amount of spread or dispersion in a data set.
   A. Quartile
   B. Percentile
   C. Standard deviation
   D. Variation

10. This pay level policy distinguishes companies from competitors by compensating employees less than most competitors.
    A. Market match policy
    B. Market lag policy
    C. Market lead policy
    D. Market share policy

11. Which of the following in **not** used to determine if the labor market that is used for a survey is relevant to a company?
    A. Where the companies are located
    B. The occupational classification of the of subjects of the survey
    C. Types of companies surveyed
    D. The method used to collect the data

12. Which two considerations were mentioned as important when deciding which compensation survey to use?
    A. Focus of the survey and the source of the survey data
    B. The length and cost of the surveys
    C. The demographics and size of the data sources used
    D. The reliability and consistency of the data

13. When a compensation professional conducts a strategic analysis and investigates industry profile, long-term market prospects, and information about their competition, they are looking at which factors?
    A. External market
    B. Internal market
    C. Industry market
    D. Strategic market

14. In strategic compensation survey considerations, the term *relevant labor market* refers to
    A. potential job openings in specific professions.
    B. the fields of potentially qualified job candidates.
    C. the number of people employed in various labor positions.
    D. the various professions that certain college degrees qualifies a person for.

15. This pay level policy distinguishes companies from competitors by compensating employees more highly than most competitors.
    A. Market match policy
    B. Market lag policy
    C. Market lead policy
    D. Market share policy

Computer Exercise 8

Working with a Salary Survey

In July Pizza Joe's participated in a local salary survey for journey level accountant positions. It is now January and you have just received the results of the salary survey. The following monthly salaries are for accountants employed in four of Pizza Joe's competitors (companies A, B, C, and D):

Company	Monthly Salary
A	$2,350
A	$2,420
A	$2,500
A	$2,750
B	$2,300
B	$2,450
B	$2,800
B	$2,900
B	$3,120
B	$3,300
B	$3,450
C	$2,650
C	$2,700
C	$2,875
C	$2,950
C	$3,200
C	$3,250
D	$1,900
D	$2,275
D	$2,400

Pizza Joe's accountants have just received annual merit increases. Their new monthly salaries are $2,704, $2,850, $2,940, and $3,020, and the pay range is $2,240 to $3,360, with a midpoint of $2,800. The accounting supervisor believes that your salaries are too low since her best accountant resigned last year to take a job that paid $200 a month more than her $2,700 a month salary.

Questions

Use the computer calculator to answer theses questions. Record your answers to questions 1 and 2 on the chart in computer exercise 8 and all the other answers on the correct Answer Sheets. (Note: For space purposes, only 16 of the above salary survey figures are listed in the software.)

1. List the survey salaries in ascending order by dragging them to the appropriate place in the salary survey column. The computer will update the salaries by increasing them by 2% (assumes a 4% annual increase rate multiplied by 6 months).

2. Calculate the following measures and enter them on Answer Sheet 2.
   A. the survey median salary (half the salaries are higher and half are lower).
   B. the survey mean (the sum of all the salaries/ the number of salaries).

3. Calculate the following measures and drag the answers to the correct place on the chart.
   A. 1st, 2nd, and 3rd Quartiles, Q1= (n+1) / 4 , Q2= twice Q1, Q3=3 times Q1, where n equals the number of entries, e.g. (16 entries +1) / 4 = 4.25, round to the 4th entry.
   B. 10th and 90th percentiles. Multiply the percent by (n+1) and divide by 100, e.g. 10th percentile for 20 entries = 10(20+1) / 100= 2.1, round to the 2nd entry.

4. Calculate the mean and median for your accountants and enter the answers on the Answer Sheet. (Use current data.)

5. Compare your salaries with the survey data and enter the answers on the Answer Sheet.
   A. Divide the survey's mean by your mean. Are you above or below the market?
   B. Calculate the survey mean after excluding the highest and lowest value (outliers). Is this value closer to your mean?

Further Study

Record your answers on the correct Answer Sheets.

F1. What is the range of your salaries? Between which percentiles do your salaries fall, e.g. between 10% and 75% (3rd quartile), between 25% (1st quartile) and 50% (2nd quartile)? Be as precise as possible using the information calculated above.

F2. Explain what adjustments, if any, are needed in your pay structure for accountants provided that Pizza Joe's wants to follow the pay policy indicated below.
- A. Market lead, with your mean in the top 75% of the market.
- B. Market match, with your mean between 45% and 55% of the market.
- C. Market lag, with your mean at or below 44% of the market.

CHAPTER 9

Building Pay Structures That Recognize Individual Contributions

Learning Objectives

1. Fundamental principles of pay structure design
2. Merit pay system structures
3. Sales incentive pay structures
4. Pay-for-knowledge structures
5. Pay structure variations—broadbanding and two-tier wage plans

Chapter Outline

I. Constructing a Pay Structure
  A. Step 1: Deciding on the Number of Pay Structures
  B. Step 2: Determining a Market Pay Line
  C. Step 3: Defining Pay Grades
  D. Step 4: Calculating Pay Ranges for Each Pay Grade
  E. Step 5: Evaluating the Results

II. Designing Merit Pay Systems
  A. Merit Increase Amounts
  B. Timing
  C. Recurring versus Nonrecurring Merit Pay Increases
  D. Present Level of Base Pay
  E. Rewarding Performance: The Merit Pay Grid
  F. Merit Pay Increases Budget

III. Designing Sales Incentive Compensation Plans
  A. Alternative Sales Compensation Plans
  B. Sales Compensation Plans and Competitive Strategy
  C. Determining Fixed Pay and the Compensation Mix

IV. Designing Pay-for-Knowledge Programs
  A. Establishing Skill Blocks
  B. Transition Matters
  C. Training and Certification

V. Pay Structure Variations
  A. Broadbanding
  B. Two-Tier Pay Structures

Key Terms

Broadbanding is a pay structure form that leads to the consolidation of existing pay grades and pay ranges into fewer wider pay grades. (p. 217)

Certification ensures that employees possess at least a minimally acceptable level of skill proficiency upon completion of a training unit. Certification methods can include work samples, oral questioning, and written tests. (p. 217)

Commission is a form of incentive compensation, based upon a percentage of the product or service selling price and the number of units sold. (p. 210)

Commission-only plan is a specific kind of sales compensation plan. Some salespeople derive their entire income through commissions. (p. 211)

Commission-plus-draw plans award sales professionals commissions and draws. (p. 210)

Common review date is the designated date when all employees receive performance evaluations. (p. 204)

Common review period is the designated period (for example, the month of June) when all employees receive performance evaluations. (p. 204)

Compa-ratios index the relative competitiveness of internal pay rates based on pay range midpoints. (p. 203)

Draw is a subsistence pay component (that is, to cover basic living expenses) in sales compensation plans. Companies usually charge draws against commissions that sales professionals are expected to earn. (p. 210)

Employee's anniversary date represents the date an employee began working for his or her present employer. Often, employees receive performance reviews on their anniversary dates. (p. 205)

Equity theory suggests an employee must regard his or her own ratio of merit increase pay to performance as similar to the ratio for other comparably performing people in the company. (p. 204)

Graduated commissions increases percentage pay rates for progressively higher sales volume in a given period. (p. 211)

Green circle rates represent pay rates for jobs that fall below the designated pay range minimums. (p. 202)

Merit pay increase budget is expressed as a percentage of the sum of employees' current base pay. (p. 207)

Midpoint pay value is the halfway mark between the range minimum and maximum rates. Midpoints generally match values along the market pay line, representing the competitive market rate determined by the analysis of compensation survey data. (p. 197)

Multiple-tiered commissions increase percentage pay rates for progressively higher sales volume in a given period only if sales exceed a predetermined level. (p. 211)

Noncash incentives complement monetary sales compensation components. Such noncash incentives as contests, recognition programs, expense reimbursement, and benefits policies can encourage sales performance and attract sales talent. (p. 213)

Nonrecoverable draws act as salary because employees are not obligated to repay the loans if they do not sell enough. (p. 210)

Nonrecurring merit increases (merit bonuses) are lump sum monetary awards based on employees' past job performance. Employees do not continue to receive nonrecurring merit increases every year. Instead, employees must earn them each time. (p. 205)

Pay compression occurs whenever a company's pay spread between newly hired or less-qualified employees and more-qualified job incumbents is small. (p. 202)

Pay grades group jobs for pay policy application. HR professionals typically group jobs into pay grades based on similar compensable factors and value. (p. 197)

Pay ranges represent the span of possible pay rates for each pay grade. Pay ranges include midpoint, minimum, and maximum pay rates. The minimum and maximum values denote the acceptable lower and upper bounds of pay for the jobs contained within particular pay grades. (p. 197)

Pay structures represent pay rate differences for jobs of unequal worth and the framework for recognizing differences in employee contributions. (p. 195)

Range spread is the difference between the maximum and the minimum pay rates of a given pay grade. (p. 200)

Recoverable draws act as company loans to employees that are carried forward indefinitely until employees sell enough (that is, earn a sufficient amount in commissions) to repay their draws. (p. 210)

Red circle rates represent pay rates that are higher than the designated pay range maximums. (p. 202)

Salary-only plan is a specific type of sales compensation plan. Sales professionals receive fixed base compensation, which does not vary with the level of units sold, increase in market share, or any other indicator of sales performance. (p. 210)

Salary-plus-bonus plans are specific type of sales compensation plans. Sales professionals receive fixed base compensation, coupled with a bonus. Bonuses usually are single payments that reward employees for achievement of specific, exceptional goals. (p. 210)

Salary-plus-commission plan is a particular type of sales compensation plan. Sales professionals receive fixed base compensation and commission. (p. 210)

Straight commission is based on the fixed percentage of the sales price of the product or service. (p. 211)

Two-tier pay structures reward newly hired employees less than established employees on either a temporary or permanent basis. (p. 219)

CHAPTER 9 REVIEW

Fill in the Blanks

Fill in the blanks with the appropriate terms.

- A. Absolute
- B. Financial self interest
- C. Compa-ratios
- D. Nonexempt positions
- E. Broadbanding
- F. Red circle
- G. Green circle
- H. Incentives
- I. Pay compression
- J. Equity theory
- K. Anniversary date
- L. Pay structures
- M. Market competitive pay rates
- N. Pay ranges
- O. Exempt positions

1. To help retain a valued employee who may receive a job offer with a competitor, a company may offer that employee what is called a _____ pay rate, which is actually greater than the maximum rate for that job's pay range.

2. Sales compensation programs can help businesses meet their objectives by aligning the _____ of sales professionals with the company's marketing objectives.

3. _____ occurs whenever a company's pay spread between newly hired or less-qualified employees and more-qualified job incumbents is small.

4. _____ pay grade point spreads are based on a set number of job evaluation points for each grade.

5. An employee who takes on a job that they are underqualified for may be paid a _____ pay rate.

6. Managers determine pay raises based on where the employee's present base pay rate is in relation to the pay ranges and the employee's _____.

7. _____ as defined by the Fair Labor Standards Act, are generally nonsupervisory, and the duties tend to be narrowly defined.

8. Pay levels that correspond with the market pay line are called _____

9. _____ are calculated by dividing an employee's pay rate by the job's pay range midpoint.

10. _____ suggests that companies should base the amount of merit pay increase on the quality of the employee's performance relative to other employees.

11. An employee's _____ is the day the employee began working for a company.

12. Unlike merit pay program increases that are generally based on subjective evaluations by an employee's supervisor, sales compensation program pay _____ that specify rewards based on meeting preestablished—often objective—levels of performance.

13. When constructing pay structures, _____ represent the vertical dimension and include midpoint, minimum, and maximum pay rates.

14. _____ is the word used to represent a pay structure that consolidates existing pay grades and ranges by reducing the levels of hierarchical corporate structures and emphasizing teamwork over individual contributions alone.

15. _____, as defined by the Fair Labor Standards Act, are generally supervisory, professional, managerial, or executive jobs that each contains a wide variety of duties.

Multiple-Choice Questions

Circle the correct answer for each question.

1. This pay value is halfway between the pay range minimum and maximum rates.
    A. Median
    B. Mean
    C. Center
    D. Midpoint

2. The Equity *Theory* suggests that
    A. if performance is equal, merit increases should be equal.
    B. if performance is equal, base pay should be made equal.
    C. if performance is equal, benefits should be equal.
    D. if base pay is equal, job responsibilities should be equal.

3. Pay compression occurs whenever a company's pay spread between newly hired or less-qualified employees and more-qualified incumbents is
    A. reduced.
    B. small.
    C. large.
    D. overlapping.

4. According to the Fair Labor Standards Act, employers do not have to give employees working on exempt jobs
    A. minimum wage
    B. vacation pay
    C. benefits
    D. overtime pay

5. Holding performance ratings constant, compensation professionals will do what to merit increase percentages as quartile ranks increase in order to control employees' progression through their pay ranges?
   A. Increase
   B. Freeze
   C. Reduce
   D. Not issue

6. When deciding on the number of pay structures, compensation professionals generally take all but which one of the following into consideration?
   A. Exempt and nonexempt pay structures
   B. The employee at that position
   C. Pay structures based on job family
   D. Pay structures based on geography

7. This compa-ratio means that the employee's pay rate falls below the competitive pay rate for the job
   A. 1.
   B. less than 1.
   C. more than 1.
   D. more than 2.

8. This commission-only plan increases percentage pay rates of commissions for all sales made in a designated period that exceeds preset sales goals.
   A. Graduated commissions
   B. Two-tiered commissions
   C. Multigraduated commissions
   D. Multiple-tiered commissions

9. This sales compensation plan awards sales professionals with advance subsistence pay that is charged against expected future sales commissions.
   A. Commission-plus-bonus
   B. Salary-plus-bonus
   C. Commission-plus-draw
   D. Salary-plus-draw

10. Which range of pay grades tends to minimize hierarchy and social distances between employees?
    A. Narrower
    B. Tiered
    C. Divergent
    D. Wider

11. When the difference between the minimum and maximum pay rates is expressed as a percentage of the difference between the two divided by the minimum it is called the
    A. range spread.
    B. pay range.
    C. pay value.
    D. pay differential.

12. Research has shown that each additional merit increase dollar does what to worker productivity?
    A. Greatly increases
    B. Has no effect
    C. Minimally increases
    D. Decreases

13. Which of the following was **not** given as something that needed to be considered when developing skill blocks?
    A. The amount of training necessary to develop the skill
    B. Individual jobs should be organized into job families
    C. Thorough job descriptions need to be developed
    D. The skills should be grouped

14. Pay compression occurs when companies fail to raise pay range minimums and maximums often because
    A. the new hires are more qualified than the incumbents.
    B. there is a large number of qualified job candidates.
    C. there is a scarcity of qualified job candidates.
    D. the economy is strong.

15. Which of the following was **not** given as one of the four main factors that managers use to develop a pay structure that will best motivate their sales professionals?
    A. Influence of the salesperson on the buying decision
    B. Number of sales leads given the sales professional
    C. Amount of nonsales activities required
    D. Noncash incentives

Computer Exercise 9

Evaluating a Merit Pay Structure

Pizza Joe's current Merit Pay Program awarded the following increases last year based on a performance ratings scale that ranges from 1 to 5:

Outstanding (5)	Excels (4)	Satisfactory (3)	Needs Improvement (2)	Unsatisfactory (1)
6%	5%	4%	2%	0%

However, the Vice-President of Human Resources is concerned that employees with salaries below their pay range midpoints are not receiving adequate raises, while those above the pay range midpoints are receiving a disproportionate share of the merit budget. Turnover for the company is relatively low, but it is highest among the most talented new employees who have salaries below the midpoint. Although your mean salaries seem to be at or above market in all your major occupations, low tenure employees who quit often report an offer of a higher salary as their reason. The V.P. of H.R. is proposing a new Merit Pay Program in H.R which would base increases on performance and position in the pay range based on quartile rankings. A friend of hers has a similar merit pay budget and uses the following merit pay grid at his company:

Performance Ratings

Quartile	5	4	3	2	1
4 th	5%	3%	2%	0	0
3 rd	6%	4%	3%	0	0
2 nd	8%	6%	4%	0	0
1 st	10%	8%	6%	0	0

For example, an employee whose pay falls in the 4 th quartile of her pay range (well above the pay range midpoint) and receives a performance rating of 5 will earn an annual pay raise equal to 5% of her current pay. Another employee whose pay falls in the 1 st quartile of his pay range (well below the pay range midpoint) and receives a performance rating of 5 will earn an annual pay raise equal to 10% of his current pay.

Before a full study is started, you have been asked to briefly review how this proposed program might affect a sample of Pizza Joe's Human Resource Specialists. The pay structure for these jobs is as follows:

Quartile 4:	$2,755 to 3,000 month
Quartile 3:	$2,505 to 2,750 month
Quartile 2:	$2,255 to 2,500 month
Quartile 1:	$2,000 to 2,250 month

You have been asked to develop scenarios for 4 hypothetical employees (Art, Bond, Clay, Door) with the following respective salaries: $2,000, $2,300, $2,600, and $2,900. They have the following respective tenure: 1 year, 3 years, 6 years, and 10 years. The salary structure will increase 5% per year in these hypothetical scenarios and no employee's salary can fall below or above the range.

Questions

For questions 1-5 enter the performance ratings for Art, Bond, Clay, and Deed in the chart in computer exercise 9. The computer will calculate the salaries for years 1, 2, and 5 under the current and proposed plans. Compare the salaries and explain the effect of the new plan given the ratings listed. Write your explanations on the Answer Sheets.

1. Assume that Art, Bond, Clay, and Deed each receive an outstanding (5) performance rating for five years. Enter the ratings in the computer chart. Compare their respective salaries under the current and proposed plans in years 1, 2, and 5. What is the effect of the new plan?

2. Assume that Art, Bond, Clay, and Deed each receive an excels (4) performance rating for five years. Compare their respective salaries under the current and proposed plans in years 1, 2, and 5. What is the effect of the new plan?

3. Assume that Art, Bond, Clay, and Deed each receive satisfactory (3) performance rating for five years. Compare their respective salaries under the current and proposed plans in years 1, 2, and 5. What is the effect of the new plan?

4. Assume that Art, Bond, Clay, and Deed receive the following respective ratings 5, 4, 3, and 2 for five years. Compare their salaries under the current and proposed plans in years 1, 2, and 5. What is the effect of the new plan?

5. Assume that Art, Bond, Clay, and Deed receive the following respective ratings 2, 3, 4, and 5 for five years. Compare their salaries under the current and proposed plans in years 1, 2, and 5. What is the effect of the new plan?

6. What are the biggest benefits and potential problems generated by the proposed plan? (Review the data from previous questions, but do not enter new data.)

Further Study

Record your answers on the correct Answer Sheets.

F1. Would you recommend that this plan be implemented as is or with changes? Explain. (Review the data from previous questions, but do not enter new data.)

F2. Design a new grid which uses different percentage increases by completing the grid in Answer Sheet F2. Assign performance ratings of your choice to employees Art, Bond, Clay, and Deed. Use the computer calculator to compute the increases under your proposal for the first year. Then enter the performance ratings in the chart in computer exercise 9 and the computer will calculate the salaries for the current and proposed plans. Compare the **first** year's salaries under the current and proposed plans with your proposal. Explain the differences in Answer Sheet F2.

CHAPTER 10
Legally Required Benefits

Learning Objectives

1. What employee benefits are legally required
2. The Social Security Act of 1935 and its mandated protection programs—unemployment insurance, benefits for dependents, and Medicare
3. Compulsory state disability laws (workers' compensation)
4. The Family & Medical Leave Act of 1993
5. Some of the implications for strategic compensation, and possible employer approaches to managing these benefits

Chapter Outline

I. **Components of Legally-Required Benefits**
   A. Social Security Act of 1935
   B. Unemployment Insurance
   C. Old Age, Survivor, and Disability Insurance (OASDI)
   D. Medicare
   E. State Compulsory Disability Laws (Workers' Compensation)
   F. Family and Medical Leave Act of 1993
II. **The Implications of Legally Required Benefits for Strategic Compensation**

Key Terms

Base period is the minimum period of time an individual must be employed before becoming eligible to receive unemployment insurance under the Social Security Act of 1935. (p. 225)

Death claims are workers' compensation claims for deaths that occur in the course of employment or that are caused by compensable injuries or occupational diseases. (p. 233)

Disability insured refers to an employee's eligibility to receive disability benefits under the Social Security Act of 1935. Eligibility depends on the worker's age and the type of disability. (p. 229)

Experience rating system establishes higher contributions (to fund unemployment insurance programs) for employers with higher incidences of unemployment. (p. 226)

Federal Employees' Compensation Act mandates workers' compensation insurance protection for federal civilian employees. (p. 232)

Federal Unemployment Tax Act (FUTA) specifies employees' and employers' tax or contribution to unemployment insurance programs required by the Social Security Act of 1935. (p. 226)

Fully insured refers to an employee's status in the retirement income program under the Social Security Act of 1935. Forty quarters of coverage lead to fully insured status. (p. 226)

Injury claims are workers' compensation claims for disabilities that have resulted from accidents such as falls, injuries from equipment use, or physical strains from heavy lifting. (p. 233)

Longshore and Harborworkers' Compensation Act mandates workers' compensation insurance protection for maritime workers. (p. 231)

Occupational disease claims are workers' compensation claims for disabilities caused by ailments associated with particular industrial trade or processes. (p. 233)

Quarters of coverage refers to each three-month period of employment during which an employee contributes to the retirement income program under the Social Security Act of 1935. (p. 226)

Supplemental insurance benefit (SUB) refers to unemployment insurance that is usually awarded to individuals who were employed in cyclical industries. This benefit supplements unemployment insurance that is required by the Social Security Act of 1935. (p. 226)

CHAPTER 10 REVIEW

Fill in the Blanks

Fill in the blanks with the appropriate terms.

A. Experience rating
B. Base period
C. Survivors' insurance
D. Medicare Part A
E. Medicare Part B
F. Cost of production
G. Injury claims

H. Federal Unemployment Tax Act
I. Family and Medical Leave Act
J. Rehabilitative services
K. State workers' compensation laws
L. Currently insured status
M. Social Security Act
N. Competitive strategy
O. Occupational disease claims

1. In an effort to recoup the costs incurred because of workers' compensation claims, many employers add those expenses to their _____ in order to pass the costs onto their clients or customers.

2. _____ provides voluntary supplementary medical insurance.

3. The _____ system, which is based on a company's unemployment history, is used to help determine the unemployment insurance tax rate the company has to pay.

4. Under *workers'* compensation laws, _____ result from disabilities caused by ailments associated with particular industrial trades and processes, such as black lung.

5. _____ and disability insurance were amendments that were added to the retirement insurance program of the Social Security Act.

6. Legally required fringe benefits do **not** directly meet the imperatives of _____.

7. The _____ is the federal legislation that requires employers to pay unemployment insurance taxes.

8. _____ provide benefits based on the principle of "liability without fault."

9. Under worker's compensation laws, _____ result from disabilities caused by accidents.

10. _____ aims to provide employees with job protection in cases of family or medical emergencies.

11. Under workers' compensation laws, _____ covers physical and vocational rehabilitation.

12. Meeting _____ entitles a beneficiary of a deceased employee to survivors' benefits under the Benefits for Dependents of the Social Security Act.

13. _____ provides compulsory hospitalization insurance.

14. To be eligible for unemployment insurance benefits, an individual must have been employed during the _____, which generally is the preceding four calendar quarters out of the last five.

15. _____ was passed as federal legislation in 1935 to help protect families from financial devastation in the event of unemployment.

Multiple-Choice Questions

Circle the correct answer for each question.

1. Coverage for in-home medical care is covered by
    A. disability insurance.
    B. Medicare Part A.
    C. Medicare Part B.
    D. retirement insurance.

2. Under the Family and Medical Leave Act, employees are entitled to _____ weeks of unpaid leave.
    A. 4
    B. 8
    C. 12
    D. 16

3. Medicare Part B covers all **but** which of the following?
    A. Hearing aids and eyeglasses
    B. Medications that cannot be self-administered
    C. Doctor consultations
    D. Diagnosis, therapy, and surgery

4. To be eligible under the Social Security disability program, the disability must be expected to last at least _____, while the benefits begin after a _____ waiting period.
    A. 24 months and 6 months
    B. 18 months and 6 months
    C. 12 months and 4 months
    D. 12 months and 6 months

5. Which of the following group of workers must pay Social Security taxes?
   A. Civilian employees of the federal government
   B. Domestic help (maids, gardeners)
   C. State and local government employees with their own retirement plans
   D. Expatriates in foreign American affiliates that are over 90% foreign owned

6. Medicare Part B covers _____ deductible.
   A. 80% of medical services after the individual pays the $200
   B. 70% of medical services after the individual pays the $100
   C. 80% of medical services after the individual pays the $100
   D. 70% of medical services after the individual pays the $200

7. Which of the following programs was **not** part of the Social Security Act of 1935?
   A. Medicaid
   B. Unemployment insurance
   C. Retirement insurance
   D. Disability benefits

8. To be eligible for benefits under the Family and Medical Leave Act, a worker must have been employed for _____.
   A. 6 months and have worked 1250 hours
   B. 6 months and have worked 1000 hours
   C. 12 months and have worked 1250 hours
   D. 12 months and have worked 1250 hours

9. Civilian employees of the federal government are covered by which workers' compensation act?
   A. Social Security Act
   B. Government Workers' Compensation Act
   C. Federal Employees Compensation Act
   D. Federal Workers' Compensation Act

10. In general, the base period for unemployment benefits is determined by how much the person earned in the _____ preceding the benefits year.
    A. first 4 out of the last 6 quarters
    B. first 6 out of the last 8 quarters
    C. first 5 out of the last 6 quarters
    D. first 4 out of the last 5 quarters

11. Employees who work for employers with less than _____ of the business are not covered under the Family and Medical Leave Act.
    A. 75 employees who live within 50 miles
    B. 50 employees who live within 50 miles
    C. 50 employees who live within 75 miles
    D. 75 employees who live within 75 miles

12. Supplemental insurance benefits are designed to help which type of workers?
    A. Unemployed
    B. Disabled
    C. Injured
    D. Those on family leave

13. According to workers' compensation laws, the employer is absolutely liable for providing benefits to employees who suffer from occupational disabilities or injuries
    A. when fault can not be determined.
    B. only if the company is at fault.
    C. regardless of fault.
    D. only when the employee is found not-at-fault.

14. To be fully insured under the Social Security retirement program, employees must either
    A. earn credit for 40 quarters of coverage, or 10 years of employment.
    B. earn credit for 10 quarters of coverage, or 20 years of employment.
    C. earn credit for 40 quarters of coverage, or 20 years of employment.
    D. earn credit for 10 quarters of coverage, or 40 years of employment.

15. The first constitutionally acceptable worker's compensation law was enacted in
    A. 1920.
    B. 1911.
    C. 1935.
    D. 1993.

Computer Exercise 10

Estimating Unemployment Benefits

Pizza Joe's top management and plant managers are at their annual planning meeting. One topic on the agenda is growth. Pizza Joe's has become so successful that current employees can no longer keep up with demand. The plant managers from Alabama and Illinois are trying to decide if they should hire additional regular employees or use temporary agency employees. Although they each would prefer to hire regular employees, they are concerned that the increased business demand may be temporary. Aggressive hiring could result in layoffs down the road. During lunch the Alabama Plant Manager calls you and asks that you determine how much unemployment benefits Pizza Joe's employees would be entitled to if layoffs become necessary. You begin investigating immediately and discover the information below. Complete the chart in the computer exercise and have it ready to fax to the manager by the end of the meeting.

State	Weekly Benefit Amount	Waiting Period
Alabama	$22 min., $180 max.	None
Illinois	$51 min.; maximums: $235 no dependents; $278 nonworking spouse; $311 one or more dependents	One week

Questions

The data above is only for use in this exercise. To calculate actual benefits one must use current data from the appropriate State. Use this chart and the computer calculator to answer these questions. Record your answers on the correct Answer Sheets and print.

1. Determine the amount of one week's unemployment benefits for a qualified person in Alabama and in Illinois under the conditions described below and calculate the difference between Illinois and Alabama weekly benefits.
    A. The person is eligible for the minimum weekly benefit.
    B. The person has no dependents and is eligible for one half the maximum weekly benefits.
    C. The person has one or more dependents and is eligible for the maximum weekly benefits.

2. Assume that a person is eligible for the full 26 weeks of benefits. Determine how

much total unemployment benefits they could receive in 26 weeks in Alabama and in Illinois under the conditions described in question 1.
- A. The person is eligible for the minimum weekly benefits.
- B. The person has no dependents and is eligible for one half the maximum weekly benefits.
- C. The person has one or more dependents and is eligible for the maximum weekly benefits.

3. What are the waiting periods in Illinois and Alabama?

Further Study

Assume that Pizza Joe's pays 6.2% of the first $7,000 earned by each employee each year in unemployment tax and that all employees earn over $7,000 in the year. Use the computer calculator and record your answers on the correct Answer Sheets and print.

F1. An entry Pizza Maker working 40 hours a week at $7.50 per hour earns $300 per week. How many weeks will Pizza Joe's have to pay the tax on an entry Pizza Maker? (That is, how many weeks does it take before an entry Pizza Maker earns at least $7,000?)

F2. How much unemployment tax will Pizza Joe's pay in one year on one employee ($7,000 X .062)? How much unemployment tax will Pizza Joe's pay in one year on 2,000 employees?

CHAPTER 11
Discretionary Benefits

Learning Objectives

1. The role of discretionary benefits in strategic compensation
2. The various kinds of protection programs
3. The different types of pay for time-not-worked
4. A variety of employee services
5. The considerations that go along with designing and planning discretionary benefits programs
6. How discretionary benefits fit with differentiation and lowest cost competitive strategies

Chapter Outline

I. **Components of Discretionary Benefits**
   A. Protection Programs
   B. Pay for Time-Not-Worked
   C. Services

II. **Laws That Guide Discretionary Fringe Compensation**
   A. Employee Retirement Income Security Act of 1974 (ERISA)
   B. Consolidated Omnibus Budget Reconciliation Act of 1985 (COBRA)
   C. Additional Pertinent Legislation

III. **Unions and Fringe Compensation**

IV. **Designing and Planning the Benefits Program**

VI. **The Implications of Discretionary Benefits for Strategic Compensation**

Key Terms

Cash balance plans are retirement plans that are designed to reduce the amount of employer contributions to an employees' retirement plan over time. (p. 248)

Coinsurance refers to the percentage of covered expenses not paid by the medical plan. (p. 249)

Commercial dental insurance provides cash benefits by reimbursing patients for out-of-pocket costs for particular dental care procedures or by paying dentists directly for patient costs. (p. 253)

Commercial insurance plans (fee-for-service plans) provide protection for three types of medical expenses—hospital expenses, surgical expenses, and physicians' charges. (p. 248)

Contributory financing employee-financed benefits are discretionary benefits to which the employer does not contribute financing. (p. 263)

Contributory pension plans require monetary contributions by the employee who will benefit from the income upon retirement. (p. 246)

Core plus option plans establish a set of benefits, such as medical insurance, as mandatory for all employees who participate in flexible benefits plans. (p. 263)

Defined benefit plans guarantee retirement benefits specified in the plan document. This benefit usually is expressed in terms of a monthly sum equal to a percentage of a participant's preretirement pay multiplied by the number of years he or she has worked for the employer. (p. 247)

Defined contribution plans require that employers and employees make annual contributions to separate retirement fund accounts established for each participating employee, based on a formula contained in the plan document. (p. 246)

Dental maintenance organizations deliver dental services through the comprehensive health care plans of many health maintenance organizations (HMOs) and preferred provider organizations (PPOs). (p. 253)

Dental service corporations owned and administered by state dental associations are nonprofit corporations of dentists. (p. 253)

Employee assistance programs (EAPs) help employees cope with personal problems that may impair their job performance, such as alcohol or drug abuse, domestic violence, the emotional impact of AIDS and other diseases, clinical depression, and eating disorders that may impair their job performance. (p. 256)

Family assistance programs help employees provide elder care and child care. Elder care provides physical, emotional, or financial assistance for aging parents, spouses, or other relatives who are not fully self-sufficient because they are too frail or disabled. Child-care programs focus on supervising preschool-age dependent children whose parents work outside the home. (p. 255)

Flexible scheduling and leave allows employees to take time off during work hours to care for relatives or react to emergencies. (p. 255)

Flexible spending accounts permit employees to pay for certain benefits expenses (such as child care) with pretax dollars. (p. 263)

Health maintenance organizations (HMOs) copayments represent nominal payments individuals make for office visits to their doctors or for prescription drugs. (p. 248)

Individual practice association, a particular kind of HMO, is a partnership or other legal entity that arranges health care services by entering into service agreements with independent physicians, health professionals, and group practices. (p. 252)

Life coverage is a type of life insurance that provides protection to employees' beneficiaries during employees' employment and into the retirement years. (p. 245)

Life insurance protects an employee's family by paying a specified amount to the employee's beneficiaries upon the employee's death. (p. 245)

Long-term disability insurance provides income benefits for extended periods of time, anywhere among six months to life. (p. 244)

Noncontributory financing implies that the company assumes total costs for discretionary benefits. (p. 263)

Noncontributory pension plans do not require employee contributions to fund retirement income. (p. 246)

Nonqualified pension plans provide less-favorable tax treatments for employers than qualified pension plans. (p. 246)

Out-of-pocket maximum is a provision in many commercial insurance plans that specifies the maximum amount a policyholder must pay per year. (p. 249)

Outplacement assistance refers to company-sponsored technical and emotional support to employees who are being laid off or terminated. (p. 256)

Pension programs provide income to individuals throughout their retirement. Companies may sometimes use early retirement programs to reduce workforce size and trim compensation expenditures. (p. 245)

Preferred provider organization (PPO) is a select group of health care providers who provide health care services to a given population at a higher level of reimbursement than under commercial insurance plans. (p. 248)

Prepaid group practices provide medical care for a set premium, rather than a fee-for-service plan. (p. 252)

Probationary period is the initial term of employment (usually fewer than six months) during which companies attempt to ensure that they have made sound hiring decisions. Often, employees are not entitled to participate in discretionary benefits programs during their probationary periods. (p. 263)

Qualified pension plans entitle employers to tax benefits from their contributions to pension plans. In general, this means that employers may take current tax deductions for contributions to fund future retirement income. (p. 246)

Self-funded insurance plans are similar to commercial insurance plans with one key difference: Companies typically draw from their own assets to fund claims when self-funded. (p. 250)

Self-insured dental plans are similar to commercial dental plans except companies fund payment for dental procedures themselves. (p. 253)

Short-term disability insurance provides income benefits for limited periods of time, usually six months or less. (p. 244)

Smoking cessation is a particular type of wellness program that stresses the negative aspects of smoking to intensive programs directed at helping individuals stop smoking. (p. 257)

Stress management is a specific kind of wellness program designed to help employees cope with many factors inside and outside of work that contribute to stress. (p. 257)

Term coverage is a type of life insurance that provides protection to employees' beneficiaries during employees' employment. (p. 245)

Transportation services represent energy efficient ways to transport employees to and from the workplace. Employers cover part or all of the transportation costs. (p. 256)

Tuition reimbursement programs promote employees' education. Under a tuition reimbursement program, an employer fully or partially reimburses an employee for expenses incurred for education or training. (p. 255)

Usual, customary, and reasonable charge deductible coinsurance is defined as being not more than the physician's usual charge; within the customary range of fees charged in the locality; and reasonable, based on the medical circumstances. Commercial insurance plans generally do not pay more than this amount. (p. 255)

Weight control and nutrition programs, a particular type of wellness program, are designed to educate employees about proper nutrition and weight loss, both of which are critical to good health. (p. 257)

Wellness programs promote employees' physical and psychological health. (p. 252)

CHAPTER 11 REVIEW
Fill in the Blanks

Fill in the blanks with the appropriate term.

A. Services
B. Long-term
C. Defined benefit plans
D. Cost shifting
E. Financed
F. Flexible
G. Flexible scheduling
H. Transportation services
I. Family assistance
J. Protection programs
K. Employee assistance
L. Tuition reimbursement programs
M. Defined contribution plans
N. Noncontributory pension plans
O. Qualified

1. _____ benefit plans allow employees to choose between two or more types of benefits.

2. _____ provide enhancements such as tuition reimbursements and day-care assistance.

3. _____ is **not** a pay-for-knowledge core compensation program because employees are allowed to take classes not related to their job responsibilities.

4. Compressed workweeks, flextime, and job sharing are examples of _____.

5. The difference between commercial and self-funded insurance plans is in how the benefits provided to policyholders are _____.

6. _____ is the practice physicians and hospitals use to offset the expenses associated with providing health care coverage to those without health protection coverage by overcharging those patients that do have health insurance.

7. The Clean Air Act Amendments of 1990 forced many urban corporations to offer _____ as part of their fringe benefit compensation packages.

8. _____ call for both the employer and employee to make annual contributions into separate pension accounts, which are then invested in things like company stocks, mutual funds, and government bonds.

9. _____ provide family benefits, promote health, and guard against income loss caused by catastrophic factors such as unemployment, disability, or serious illnesses.

10. A _____ pension plan allows employers tax breaks on their contributions and employees favorable tax treatment when they retire and receive their benefits.

11. _____ disability is defined as the inability of an employee to engage in any occupation for which the employee is qualified.

12. _____ are set up to guarantee the amount of benefits the employees will receive upon retirement.

13. _____ help employees to provide elder and child care.

14. _____ help employees cope with personal problems that may impair their job performance.

15. _____ are pension programs that receive contributions only from the employer.

Multiple-Choice Questions

Circle the correct answer for each question.

1. This federal legislation legitimized collective bargaining for employee benefits.
   A. Fair Labor Standards Act
   B. National Labor Relations Act
   C. National Labor Bargaining Act
   D. National Collective Bargaining Act

2. Long-term disability benefits usually cover up to how long?
   A. 100% of the employee's pay after a 6-month period
   B. 100% of the employee's pay after a 9-month period
   C. 70% of the employee's pay after a 6-month period
   D. 70% of the employee's pay after a 9-month period

3. This federal legislation was established to regulate the establishment and implementation of such fringe benefits programs as medical, life, and disability programs.
   A. Fair Labor Standards Act
   B. Employee Retirement Income Security Act
   C. Consolidated Omnibus Budget Reconciliation Act
   D. Employee Compensation Act

4. This federal legislation was established to provide employees with the opportunity to temporarily continue receiving their employer-sponsored medical care insurance after changes in their employment status.
   A. Fair Labor Standards Act
   B. Employee Retirement Income Security Act
   C. Consolidated Omnibus Budget Reconciliation Act
   D. Employee Compensation Act

5. Which of the following pay for time-not-worked benefit was **not** found in most private or governmental compensation benefits packages in 1992?
   A. Funeral leave
   B. Jury duty leave
   C. Military leave
   D. Clean-up, preparation, & travel time leave

6. Under this HMO plan, physicians qualify as providers by meeting quality standards, agreeing to follow cost containment procedures implemented by this type of HMO, and to accept its reimbursement structure. In return, this HMO group guarantees the physicians certain patient loads by furnishing employees with financial incentives to use this type of HMO plan.
   A. Prepaid group practice
   B. Preferred provider organizations
   C. Individual practice associations
   D. Prepaid provider organizations

7. Short-term disability insurance usually provides benefits for up to how many months?
   A. 3
   B. 6
   C. 9
   D. 12

8. This program is offered, in some companies, as a group of services available to employees who are being laid off.
   A. Job placement assistance
   B. Transition assistance
   C. Outplacement assistance
   D. Involuntary layoff assistance

9. Which of the following are the two minimum requirements for eligibility under ERISA?
   A. Employee at least 18 years of age and have worked 1000 hours
   B. Employee at least 21 years of age and have worked 1000 hours
   C. Employee at least 18 years of age and have worked 1500 hours
   D. Employee at least 18 years of age and have worked 1500 hours

10. In the 1940s and 1950s, this term referred to anything the company offered an employee, over and above a base pay, that was not federally mandated, yet enhanced the social or intellectual life of the employee.
    A. Social benefits
    B. Incentive benefits
    C. Welfare practices
    D. Family benefits

11. Stress management, stop smoking, and weight control plans are considered part of which type of discretionary benefit?
    A. Outplacement services
    B. Family assistance programs
    C. Wellness programs
    D. Alternative health programs

12. All but one of the following are considered broad categories of discretionary benefits.
    A. Bonuses
    B. Protection programs
    C. Pay for time-not-worked
    D. Services

13. This type of dental insurance provider is a nonprofit corporation that is administered by state dental associations where the patient must pay the difference between the fixed reimbursement amount and the actual amount the dentist charges.
    A. Commercial dental insurance
    B. Dental maintenance organizations
    C. Self-insured dental plans
    D. Dental service corporations

14. Long-term disability insurance will provide benefits for how long?
    A. 25 years
    B. Until retirement age
    C. 20 years
    D. Life

15. Companies must offer HMO's if they
    A. are subject to the minimum wage provisions of the Fair Labor Standards Act.
    B. have over 20 employees.
    C. are unionized with over 50 employees.
    D. have employees with children.

Computer Exercise 11

Costing Discretionary Benefits

Pizza Joe's is considering enhancing their current vacation benefits. The current plan provides the following paid vacation days to full-time employees based on employee service:

> 1 week after 1 year of service
> 2 weeks after 3 years of service
> 3 weeks after 10 years of service

You know that Pizza Joe's has received numerous complaints from employees and management that 2 weeks of vacation is insufficient for employees with over 5 years of service. You have just discovered in the U.S. Bureau of Labor Statistics report on *Employee Benefits in Medium and Large Private Establishments* that half the firms provide 3 weeks or more vacation to employees after 5 years of service. The Director of Compensation has asked you to estimate the cost of providing 3 weeks vacation after 5 years, 6 years, or 7 years of service. You discover that 400 employees have between 5 and 9 years of service and that 80 employees fall into each category, i.e. 80 have 5 years of service, 80 have 6 years, etc. You estimate that direct payroll costs of wages and salaries for these 400 employees equals 10 million dollars and current benefits costs equal 3.8 million dollars. Estimate the cost of these alternative programs under the conditions described below.

Questions

Use the computer calculator to answer theses questions. Record your answers on the correct Answer Sheets, complete the exercise, and print.

1. Follow the steps below to calculate the direct payroll costs for the proposals above.
    - A. What is the average annual earnings for each of these employees? (Hint: this will be the direct payroll divided by the total employees.)
    - B. What is the average weekly earnings for these employees?
    - C. Multiply the average weekly earnings by the number of employees who meet the service requirement to determine the direct payroll costs for the additional paid time not worked. Give the cost of adding one week of vacation to all employees with 5 or more years of service, with 6 or more years of service, and with 7 or more years of service.

2. Each of these proposals would increase the benefit costs for these 400 employees. Determine the percentage increase in benefit costs which would result from each

proposal by dividing the cost increases calculated in question 1C by $3,800,000 and multiplying by 100.

    A.   If all employees with 5 or more years of service receive an extra week of vacation.

    B.   If all employees with 6 or more years of service receive an extra week of vacation.

    C.   If all employees with 7 or more years of service receive an extra week of vacation.

3. Calculate the measures below assuming that 3 weeks vacation is given to all employees with 5 or more years of service.

    A.   How much would benefits cost? (Add the increase calculated in question 1C to $3.8 million.)

    B.   Benefit costs would represent what percent of direct payroll? (Divide 3A by $10 million and multiply by 100.)

Further Study

F1. If Pizza Joe's gives the extra week of vacation to the 400 employees with 5 or more years of service, how much would it cost them in direct pay and benefit costs to replace the hours lost? Assume that they paid the same rate of pay (10 million for 400 employees) and benefit costs (3.8 million for 400 employees). (Add these direct payroll and benefit costs together and divide the sum by 52 to get the cost of a one week vacation for this entire group.

CHAPTER 12
International Compensation

Learning Objectives

1. Competitive strategies and how international activities fit in
2. How globalization affects HR departments
3. Methods for setting expatriates' base pay
4. Incentive compensation for expatriates
5. Fringe compensation for expatriates
6. The balance sheet approach
7. Repatriation issues
8. Compensation issues for HCNs and TCNs

Chapter Outline

I. **Competitive Strategies and How International Activities Fit In**
   A. Lowest Cost Producers' Relocation to Cheaper Production Areas
   B. Differentiation and the Search for New Global Markets

II. **How Globalization Is Affecting HR Departments**
   A. Selection and Training
   B. The Complexity of International Compensation Programs

III. **Preliminary Considerations**
   A. Host-Country Nationals (HCNs) Third-Country Nationals (TCNs), and Expatriates: Definitions and Relevance
   B. Term of International Assignment
   C. Staff Mobility
   D. Equity: Pay Referent Groups

IV. **Components of International Compensation Programs**
   A. Base Pay
   B. Fringe Benefits

V. **Setting Base Pay for U.S. Expatriates**
   A. Methods for Setting Base Pay
      1. Home-country-based method
      2. Host-country-based method
      3. Headquarters-based method

    B. Purchasing Power
        1. Currency stabilization
        2. Inflation

VI. Incentive Compensation for U.S. Expatriates

    A. Foreign Service Premiums
    B. Hardship Allowances
    C. Mobility Premiums

VII. Establishing Fringe Compensation for U.S. Expatriates

    A. Standard Benefits for U.S. Expatriates
        1. Protection programs
        2. Pay for time-not-worked
    B. Enhanced Benefits for U.S. Expatriates
        1. Relocation assistance
        2. Education reimbursement for expatriate's children
        3. Home leave benefits and travel reimbursements
        4. Rest and relaxation leave and allowance

VIII. Balance Sheet Approach

    A. Housing and Utilities
    B. Goods and Services
    C. Discretionary Income
    D. Tax Considerations
        1. Choosing between IRC Section 901 and IRC Section 911
        2. Employer Considerations: Tax protection and tax equalization

IX. Repatriation Pay Issues

    A. Compensation Issues for HCNs
    B. Compensation Issues for TCNs

Key Terms

Balance sheet approach to designing expatriate compensation packages that attempts to provide expatriates with the standard of living they are used to in the United States. (p. 286)

Bona fide foreign residence criterion is one of the two criteria that must be met to qualify an expatriate's living quarters as a tax home for the IRC Section 911 income exclusion. (p. 290)

Discretionary income covers a variety of financial obligations expatriates remain responsible for in the United States. (p. 288)

Exchange rate is the rate one country's currency can be exchanged for another country's currency. (p. 280)

Expatriates are U.S. citizens employed in U.S. companies with work assignments outside the United States. (p. 277)

Foreign service premiums are monetary payments, above their regular base pay, awarded to expatriates for accepting an assignment overseas. (p. 281)

Goods and services allowances compensate expatriates for the difference between goods and service costs in the United States and in the host country. (p. 288)

Hardship allowance compensates expatriates for their sacrifices while on assignment. (p. 281)

Headquarters-based method compensates all employees according to the pay scales used at the MNC's headquarters. (p. 279)

Home-country-based method compensates expatriates for the amount they would receive if they were performing similar work in the United States. (p. 279)

Home leave benefits enable expatriates to take paid time off in the United States to help them adjust to their foreign assignments and to maintain contact with family and friends. (p. 285)

Host-country-based method compensates expatriates based on the host-countries' pay scales. (p. 279)

Host-country nationals (HCNs) are foreign national citizens who work in U.S. companies' branch offices or manufacturing plants in the workers' home countries. (p. 277)

Hypothetical tax is used by MNCs to estimate taxes owed to the IRS by expatriates to reduce the effects of *double taxation* (p. 292)

Indexes of living costs abroad compare the costs (U.S. dollars) of goods and services (excluding education) expatriates purchase in the host country to the cost of comparable goods and services purchased in the Washington, D.C. area. Companies use these indexes to determine appropriate goods and service allowances. (p. 288)

Inflation is the increase in prices for consumer goods and services. Inflation erodes the purchasing power of currency. (p. 280)

IRC Section 901 allows expatriates to credit foreign income taxes against their U.S. income liability. (p. 289)

IRC Section 911 permits eligible expatriates to exclude as much as $70,000 of foreign earned income, and a housing allowance, from their U.S. tax obligation. (p. 290)

Mobility premiums reward employees for moving from one work assignment to another. (p. 281)

North American Free Trade Agreement (NAFTA) is a government mandate designed to reduce trade barriers among Mexico, Canada, and the United States and to remove barriers to investment among these three countries. (p. 275)

Physical foreign presence criterion one of two criteria that must be met to qualify an expatriate's living quarters as a tax home for the IRC Section 911 income exclusion. (p. 290)

Quarters allowances are amounts calculated by the U.S. State Department designed to allow MNCs to determine how much extra it will cost to allow expatriates standard-of-living conditions comparable to the ones they are accustomed to in the United States (p. 287)

Relocation assistance payments cover expatriates' expenses to relocate to foreign posts. (p. 285)

Repatriation is the process of making the transition from an international assignment and living abroad to a domestic employment assignment and living in the United States again. (p. 276)

Rest and relaxation leave and allowances provide expatriates, assigned to hardship locations, paid time off. Rest and relaxation leave benefits differ from standard vacation benefits because companies designate where expatriates may spend their time. (p. 285)

Tax equalization is one of two approaches (the other is tax protection) used by MNCs to provide expatriates tax allowances and avoid *double taxation*. This approach is used when the expatriates' actual income tax obligations are less that the hypothetical tax they were subjected to. (p. 293)

Tax protection is one of two approaches (the other is tax equalization) used by MNCs to provide expatriates tax allowances and avoid *double taxation*. This approach is used when the expatriates' actual income tax obligations are greater than the hypothetical tax they were subjected to. (p. 292)

Third-country nationals (TCNs) are foreign national citizens who work in a U.S. company's branch office or manufacturing plant in a country other than their home country or in the United States (p. 277)

CHAPTER 12 REVIEW

Fill in the Blanks

Fill in the blanks with the appropriate terms.

A. Host-country based
B. Tax equalization
C. Repatriation
D. Discretionary income
E. Physical foreign presence
F. Host-country national
G. Inflation
H. Bona fide foreign residence
I. Tax protection
J. Tax effectiveness
K. Headquarters
L. Home-country
M. Staff mobility
N. Third-country national
O. Balance sheet approach

1. _____ is the process of making the transition back to living in the United States after having worked overseas.

2. A Chinese citizen working for an American company in Poland would be called a _____.

3. _____ is a term used to describe an expatriate's willingness to go from one foreign assignment to another.

4. The _____ based compensation method is the one most appropriate to use where the assignments are of a long duration.

5. The _____ to determining expatriates' compensation packages is designed to protect each expatriate's standard-of-living and to help MNCs control their costs.

6. Two key factors influence purchasing power—the stability of local currency and _____.

7. The _____ based method of calculating expatriate base pay compensates expatriates the amount they would receive if they were performing similar work in the United States.

8. The _____ based compensation method is the one most appropriate to use when expatriates go from one foreign assignment to another.

9. When using the balance sheet approach, _____ is generally the tax method used when the actual U.S. income tax is less than the hypothetical tax.

10. Total remuneration, benefit adequacy, _____, and recognition of local customs and practices should to be taken into consideration when designing international fringe benefits programs.

11. One of the criteria of the _____ test for determining an expatriate's "tax home" requires the expatriate to be present in the host country for 330 days—during a 12-month period.

12. _____ covers a variety of financial obligations in the United States for which expatriates remain responsible while on overseas assignments.

13. One of the criteria of the _____ test for determining an expatriate's "tax home" requires the expatriate intend to be involved in the social life and culture of the host country.

14. When using the balance sheet approach, _____ is generally the tax method used when the actual income tax is greater than the hypothetical tax.

15. A Russian employee, working for a U.S. MNC in Moscow, is considered a _____

Multiple-Choice Questions

Circle the correct answer for each question.

1. This benefit is designed to compensate expatriates for exceptionally difficult working and living conditions in certain host-country assignments.
    A. Hardcore allowances
    B. Hardtime allowances
    C. Hardship allowances
    D. Hard-living allowances

2. Under the balance sheet approach, companies can choose between which two approaches to provide expatriates with income tax allowances?
    A. Tax allocation and tax protection
    B. Tax equalization and tax deferment
    C. Tax protection and tax equalization
    D. Tax deferment and tax protection

3. The three main types of incentives used to compensate expatriates are
    A. foreign service premiums, hardship allowances, and mobility premiums.
    B. foreign service premiums, hardship allowances, and repatriation premiums.
    C. hardship allowances, repatriation premiums, and mobility premiums.
    D. foreign service premiums, repatriation premiums, and mobility premiums.

4. Which of the following is **not** considered a criterion for determining hardship?
   A. Notably unhealthy living conditions
   B. Dangerous conditions affecting physical and/or mental well-being
   C. Inability to bring family members
   D. Extraordinarily difficult living conditions

5. An American working in an American company's overseas affiliate is called a/an
   A. repatriate.
   B. expatriate.
   C. compatriate.
   D. patriate.

6. Standard expatriate fringe compensation packages contain at least these two programs.
   A. Pay for-time-worked and protection programs
   B. Provision programs and pay-for-time-not-worked
   C. Provision programs and pay-for-time-worked
   D. Pay for time-not-worked and protection programs

7. The three main components of an expatriate compensation package are core compensation, fringe compensation, and
   A. enriched benefits.
   B. entitlement benefits.
   C. enhanced benefits.
   D. extended benefits.

8. International compensation programs must be designed to meet the needs of all the following designations of employees **except**
   A. third-world nationals.
   B. host-country nationals.
   C. third-country nationals.
   D. expatriates.

9. A main reason cited for lower labor costs in Mexico and China is that these countries place
   A. a lower value on an individual's standard of living.
   B. a lower value on an individual's cost of living.
   C. a lower value on individual employee rights.
   D. a lower value on work ethic.

10. Which of the following was **not** mentioned as an enhanced benefit for expatriates?

    A. Home leave and travel reimbursements
    B. Relocation assistance
    C. Rest and relaxation reimbursement
    D. Host-country holiday pay

11. Rest and relaxation (R & R) leave benefits differ from vacation pay in that

    A. vacation time is for a shorter period.
    B. R & R leave must be taken in a designated location.
    C. R & R reimbursement amount is less.
    D. R & R can only be taken at certain times.

12. The balance sheet approach compares the cost of and all **but** one of the following expenditures.

    A. Hypothetical taxes
    B. Housing
    C. Goods and services
    D. Discretionary income

13. International compensation programs pose several challenges for the HR professionals in most MNCs. Which of the following is **not** considered one of them?

    A. Minimizing the financial risks to the expatriates
    B. Preparing for smooth repatriation transitions
    C. Encouraging employees to accept overseas assignments
    D. Removing the international benefits once the employee repatriates

14. These two sections of the *Internal Revenue Code* enable expatriates to minimize double taxation liability.

    A. IRC Sections 901 and 911
    B. IRC Sections 191 and 901
    C. IRC Sections 119 and 191
    D. IRC Sections 191 and 911

15. International compensation packages are mainly based on all **but** which of the following?

    A. The number of expatriates at the overseas operation
    B. The length of the overseas assignment
    C. Staff mobility
    D. Equity: Pay referent groups

Computer Exercise 12

International Compensation: Preparing a Balance Sheet

Pizza Joe's is considering establishing a foreign plant to meet the growing international demand for frozen pizza. They have narrowed the search to Tokyo, Japan or Melbourne, Australia, but have not made a final decision. Eventually, they plan to send one U.S. mid-level manager (expatriate) to the location chosen to establish the plant. The officers have requested information on all aspects of the expansion program. You have been asked to prepare a balance sheet for both locations in order to estimate the cost of allowances. The officers plan to pay the expatriate allowances to cover the difference between costs in the U.S. and in the foreign location. You find the housing and utility allowance and the goods and services allowance (Index of Living Costs) in the *U.S. Department of State Indexes of Living Costs Abroad, Quarters Allowances, and Hardship Differentials* and the tax rates in business reference books. You discover the following information for Melbourne and Tokyo:

Location	Housing Allowance	Index of Living Costs	Tax Rate
Melbourne, Australia		130	47%
Family	$16,400		
Single	$15,400		
Tokyo, Japan		233	35%
Family	$81,000		
Single	$78,000		

For the purpose of this exercise assume that your mid-level manager makes $75,000 per year and has the following annual expenses in the U.S.: $32,000 in housing and utilities, $10,000 in goods and services, $21,000 in taxes ($75,000 at 28%), and $12,000 in discretionary income.

Questions

Use the computer calculator to complete the balance sheet in the computer exercise. Assume that the manager has the expenses listed above. Complete a balance sheet for each scenario below and print.

1. A married manager is working in Melbourne, Australia.

2. A single manager is working in Melbourne, Australia.

3. A married manager is working in Tokyo, Japan.

4. A single manager is working in Tokyo, Japan.

If you need help, follow the steps below.

A. Enter the person's annual expenses in the U.S. column.
B. Enter the housing allowance in the allowance column.
C. Calculate the U. S. equivalent expense for housing by adding the U.S. housing and utility expenses to the housing allowance. Enter the sum in the U.S. equivalent column.
D. Calculate the U. S. equivalent expense for goods and services by multiplying the U.S. goods and services expenses by the index of living costs divided by 100, e.g. $10,000 X 1.30. Enter the result in the U.S. equivalent column.
E. Calculate the allowance for goods and services by subtracting the U.S. goods and services expenses from the U.S. equivalent goods and services expenses. Enter the result under the goods and services allowance.
F. Estimate the foreign taxes by multiplying $75,000 times the tax rate, e.g. 75,000 X .47. Enter the result under U.S. equivalent taxes. (Note: Actual taxes are complex. These simplified figures are provided for illustrative purposes only.)
G. Calculate the allowance for taxes by subtracting the U.S. tax expenses from the U.S. equivalent tax expense. Enter the result under taxes allowance.
H. U.S. and U.S. equivalent discretionary income should be the same since this number represents the manager's ongoing financial commitments in the U.S. Enter zero under the allowance column.

Further Study

The stability of local currency and inflation both affect the expatriate's purchasing power during the assignment. In addition, allowances may be based on surveys which were conducted 6 to 24 months prior to the assignment. With this in mind, complete a balance sheet for each scenario below and print.

F1. A married manager is working in Melbourne, Australia. The housing allowance and index of cost of living should be 20% higher to reflect actual expenses.

F2. A single manager is working in Tokyo, Japan. The above housing allowance and index of cost of living overstate real expenses. Reduce them each by 25%.

CHAPTER 13
Compensating Executives

Learning Objectives

1. Components of executive core compensation
2. Components of executive fringe compensation
3. Principles and processes of setting executive compensation
4. Executive compensation disclosure rules
5. The executive compensation controversy: Are U.S. executives paid too much?

Chapter Outline

I. **Defining Executive Status**
   A. Who Are Executives?
   B. Key Employees

II. **Executive Compensation Packages**
   A. Components of Current Core Compensation
   B. Components of Deferred Core Compensation: Stock Compensation
   C. Components of Deferred Core Compensation: The Golden Parachute
   D. Components of Fringe Compensation: Enhanced Protection Program Benefits and Perquisites

III. **Principles and Processes for Setting Executive Compensation**
   A. The Key Players in Setting Executive Compensation
   B. Theoretical Explanations for Setting Executive Compensation

IV. **Executive Compensation Disclosure Rules**

V. **Executive Compensation: Are U.S. Executives Paid Too Much?**
   A. Comparison between Executive Compensation and Compensation for Other Worker Groups
   B. A Strategic Question: Is Pay Commensurate with Performance?
   C. An Ethical Consideration: Is Executive Compensation Fair?
   D. International Competitiveness

Key Terms

Agency theory provides an explanation of executive compensation determination based on the relationship between company owners (shareholders) and agents (executives). (p. 311)

Board of Directors represents shareholders' interests, in compensation negotiations, by weighing the pros and cons of top executives' decisions. Members include chief executive officers and top executives of other successful companies, distinguished community leaders, well-regarded professionals (i.e., physicians, attorneys), and a few of the company's top-level executives. (p. 310)

Capital gains is the difference between the company stock price at the time of purchase and the lower stock price at the time an executive received the stock options. (p. 305)

Compensation committee contains Board of Directors members within and outside a company. Compensation committees review an executive compensation consultant's alternate recommendations for compensation packages, discuss the assets and liabilities of the recommendations, and recommend the consultant's best proposal to the Board of Directors for their consideration. (p. 310)

Deferred compensation refers to an agreement between an employee and a company to render payments to an employee at a future date. Deferred compensation is a hallmark of executive compensation packages. (p. 304)

Derivative lawsuits represent legal action that is initiated by company shareholders claiming that executive compensation is excessive. (p. 314)

Discretionary bonuses are awarded to executives on an elective basis, by the Board of Directors. The Board of Directors weigh four factors in determining discretionary bonus amounts—company profits, the financial condition of the company, business conditions, and prospects for the future. (p. 303)

Executive compensation consultants propose recommendations to chief executive officers and Board of Directors members for alternate executive compensation packages. (p. 309)

Golden parachute, a kind of executive deferred compensation, provides pay and benefits to executives following their termination resulting from a change in ownership or a corporate takeover. (p. 306)

Incentive stock options entitle executives to purchase their companies' stock in the future at a predetermined price. Usually, the predetermined price equals the stock price at the time an executive receives the stock options. Incentive stock options entitle executives to favorable tax treatment. (p. 305)

Key employee, as defined by the Internal Revenue Service, is an employee who, at any time during the current year or any of the four preceding years, is one of 10 employees owning the largest percentages of the company, or an employee who owns more than 5% of the company, or an employee who earns more than $150,000 per year and owns more than 1% of the company. (p. 301)

Nonstatutory stock options, a kind of executive deferred compensation, entitles executives to purchase their companies' stock in the future at a predetermined price. Usually, the predetermined price equals the stock price at the time an executive receives the stock options. Nonstatutory stock options do not entitle executives to favorable tax treatment. (p. 305)

Performance-contingent bonuses awarded to executives are based on the attainment of such specific performance criteria as market share attainment. (p. 303)

Perquisites (perks) are benefits offered exclusively to executives, for example, country club memberships. (p. 307)

Phantom stock, a type of executive deferred compensation, is an arrangement whereby boards of directors compensate executives with hypothetical company stocks rather than actual shares of company stock. Phantom stock plans are similar to restricted stock plans because executives must meet specific conditions before they can convert these phantom shares into real shares of company stock. (p. 306)

Predetermined allocation bonuses are awarded to executives and are based on a fixed formula. Often, a company's profit is the main determinant of the bonus amounts. (p. 303)

Restricted stock, a type of executive deferred compensation, requires that executives do not have any ownership control over the disposition of the stock for a predetermined period, oftentimes, 5 to 10 years. (p. 306)

Securities and Exchange Commission (SEC) is a nonpartisan, quasi-judicial federal government agency with responsibility for administering federal securities laws. (p. 312)

Securities Exchange Act of 1934 applies to the disclosure of executive compensation. (p. 312)

Social comparison theory provides an explanation for executive compensation determination based on the tendency for Board of Directors to offer executive compensation packages that are similar to the executive compensation packages in peer companies. (p. 311)

Stock appreciation rights, a type of executive deferred compensation, provide executives income at the end of a designated period, much as with restricted stock options. However, executives never have to exercise their stock rights to receive income. The company simply awards payment to executives based on the difference in stock price between the time the company granted the stock rights at fair market value to the end of the designated period, permitting the executives to keep the stock. (p. 306)

Supplemental life insurance protection represents additional life insurance protection offered exclusively to executives. Companies design executives' supplemental life insurance protection to increase the value of executives' estates, bequeathed to designated beneficiaries (usually, family members) upon their death and to provide greater benefits than standard plans usually allow. (p. 307)

Supplemental retirement plans, offered to executives, are designed to restore benefits restricted under qualified plans. (p. 307)

Target plan bonuses are awarded to executives and based on executives' performance. Executives do not receive bonuses unless their performance exceeds minimally acceptable standards. (p. 309)

Tournament theory provides an explanation for executive compensation determination based on substantially greater competition for high-ranking jobs. Lucrative chief executive compensation packages represent the prize to those who win the competition by becoming chief executives. (p. 311)

CHAPTER 13 REVIEW

Fill in the Blanks

Fill in the blanks with the appropriate terms.

A. Capital gains
B. Perquisites
C. Target plan
D. Tournament
E. Nonstatutory
F. Bonuses
G. Golden parachutes
H. Deferred compensation
I. Enhanced protection program
J. Derivative
K. Agency
L. Restricted
M. Short-term incentives
N. Performance-contingent
O. Stock options

1. _____ are perks that are fringe benefits for executives exclusively.

2. The _____ stock option plan in similar to the incentive stock plan except that it does not qualify for favorable tax treatment.

3. The _____ theory of setting executive compensation packages is similar to a winner-take-all, single-elimination sports challenge.

4. Achieving predetermined goals are used to reward executives with _____ bonuses.

5. The difference between the _____ bonuses and predetermined allocation bonuses is that these bonus amounts are fixed, regardless of corporate performance, in a predetermined allocation amount.

6. _____ are awarded to executives to recognize their progress toward fulfilling competitive strategy goals.

7. _____ is designed to create a sense of ownership by aligning the executive's interests with those of the owners or shareholders.

8. _____ are the main components of an executive's deferred compensation package.

9. _____ is the difference between the stock price at the time of purchase and the lower stock price at the time an executive receives the stock option.

10. _____ provide pay and benefits to executives after their termination resulting from either a change in ownership or a corporate takeover.

11. _____ represent single pay-for-performance payments to reward employees for achievement of exceptional goals.

12. Supplemental life insurance and supplemental retirement plans are part of an executive's _____ package.

13. If shareholders think an executive's compensation package is too excessive; they can bring a _____ lawsuit on behalf of the corporation before the SEC.

14. Issuing _____ stock options is a common type of long-term compensation component that does not allow executives to take over ownership for a defined period of time.

15. The _____ theory of setting executive compensation is centered around shareholders delegating that authority to top executives.

Multiple-Choice Questions

Circle the correct answer for each question.

1. An employee's purchase of stock using stock options is called

    A. exercise of stock grant.
    B. disposition.
    C. stock granting.
    D. stock optioning.

2. All **but** one of the following is used by the IRS to define a key employee.

    A. Makes decisions that affect the entire company
    B. One of 10 employees owning the largest percentages of the company
    C. An employee who owns more than 5% of the company
    D. An employee who earns more than $150,000 per year and owns more than 1% of the company

3. Which of the following is not considered a bonus available to most executives?

    A. Performance-contingent bonus
    B. Predetermined allocation bonus
    C. Discretionary bonus
    D. Stock option bonus

4. Executive current core compensation packages contains all the following except

    A. short-term incentives.
    B. annual bonuses.
    C. annual base pay.
    D. golden parachute.

5. The SEC Summary Compensation Table discloses compensation information for the CEO and the ___.

   A. four most highly paid executives over a three-year period
   B. three most highly paid executives over a four-year period
   C. four most highly paid executives over a four-year period
   D. four most highly paid executives over a five-year period

6. The sale of stock by a stockholder is called

   A. stock option.
   B. disposition.
   C. stock grant.
   D. exercise of stock grant.

7. Which of the following is **not** one of the three alternative theories used to explain the principles and processes for setting executive compensation?

   A. Agency theory
   B. Compensation security theory
   C. Tournament theory
   D. Social comparison theory

8. This type of deferred stock compensation plan requires executives to pay income taxes on the difference between the discounted stock price and the stock's fair market value at the time of the stock grant.

   A. Incentive stock options
   B. Nonstatutory stock options
   C. Phantom stock options
   D. Discount stock options

9. This deferred stock compensation plan provides executives with an income at the end of a designated period without having to exercise their stock rights to receive income.

   A. Restricted stock options
   B. Nonstatutory stock options
   C. Stock appreciation rights
   D. Phantom stock rights

10. This type of deferred stock compensation plan is similar to the nonstatutory stock option plan except that in this plan companies grant stock options at rates far below the stock's fair market value on the date the option is granted.

    A. Incentive stock options
    B. Nonstatutory stock options
    C. Phantom stock options
    D. Discount stock options

11. Two of the components of enhanced protection programs that distinguish the executive programs from other employees' programs are supplemental

    A. health insurance and life insurance.
    B. health insurance and retirement benefits.
    C. retirement benefits and life insurance.
    D. retirement and disability insurance.

12. The Family and Medical Leave Act does not guarantee the same job upon returning from leave to what percent of the highest-paid salaried employees?

    A. 10%
    B. 15%
    C. 20%
    D. 25%

13. Executive compensation packages include all the following except

    A. current or annual core compensation.
    B. deferred core compensation.
    C. deferred fringe compensation.
    D. fringe compensation.

14. Company profits, the company's financial condition, business conditions, and the prospects for future business are all factors in determining which type of executive bonus?

    A. Target plan
    B. Discretionary
    C. Predetermined allocation
    D. Performance-contingent

15. This type of deferred stock compensation plan occurs when the Board of Directors compensates executives with hypothetical company stocks rather than actual shares.

    A. Incentive stock options
    B. Nonstatutory stock options
    C. Phantom stock options
    D. Discount stock options

Computer Exercise 13

Analyzing Executive Compensation

Historically Pizza Joe's has paid officers a salary and an annual bonus. However, this year they are adding incentive stock options to the executive compensation package. The officers were granted the stock options below at fair market value. They will be eligible to buy Pizza Joe's stock in 5 years at today's price of twenty dollars a share. You have been asked to analyze the executive compensation package in light of this addition. Below is a chart of each officer's most recent performance rating, and total current compensation (i.e., current salary and bonus).

Positions	Stock Grant	Ratings	Total Current Compensation Salary	Bonus
I. Bigby CEO & President	10,000	NA	$600,000	$100,000
W. Onabee Executive V.P.	5,000	4	$400,000	$50,000
A. Mann V.P. Operations	4,000	5	$350,000	$70,000
M. Trader V.P. Marketing	4,000	4	$320,000	$40,000
F. Money V.P. Finance	2,000	4	$300,000	$40,000
S. Plotter V.P. Planning	2,000	4	$200,000	$25,000
R. Crew V.P. H. R.	2,000	5	$175,000	$35,000

Questions

Use the computer calculator to answer theses questions. Record your answers on the correct Answer Sheets, complete the exercise, and print.

1. Determine the percentage of total compensation currently paid in base salary and as a bonus for each officer, e.g. Bigby's $600,000 base divided by $700,000 total, and multiplied by 100 equals his percent paid in base salary.

2. Determine how much each officer could make after 5 years by exercising his or her stock options at the price below. To calculate the gain per share, subtract $20.00 from the price below. Multiply the gain per share by the number of shares each officer was granted.
   A. $25.00
   B. $30.00
   C. $35.00
   D. $40.00

3. Assume that at the end of 5 years the stock price is $40 per share and all the officers exercise their shares. Enter your answers on Answer Sheet 3.
   A.   Enter each officer's total compensation (add the 5th year salary and bonus from the computer chart to the officers' gains from question 2D).
   B.   Enter the percentage of total compensation paid to each officer in base salary (base salary / total compensation, multiplied by 100).
   C.   Enter the percentage of total compensation paid to each officer as a bonus.
   D.   Enter the percentage of total compensation received by each officer in stock gains (gain from 2D / total compensation, multiplied by 100).

Further Study

F1. Pizza Joe's entry Pizza Maker currently makes $7.50 per hour ($15,600 per year). Determine what percentage of the CEO's total annual compensation this person will make in the following situations and record your answers on the Answer Sheet.
   A.   At the beginning of this exercise ($15,600 / $700,000).
   B.   After 5 years, assuming that the Pizza Maker's earnings and the CEO's salary and bonuses increased by 5% per year, and Pizza Joe's stock is $40.00 per share. (Divide the Pizza Maker's earnings ($20,905) by the CEO's total compensation from question 3A, and multiply by 100.)

CHAPTER 14

Compensating the Flexible Workforce: Contingent Employees and Flexible Work Schedules

Learning Objectives

1. Various groups of contingent workers and the reasons for U.S. employers' increased reliance on them
2. Core and fringe compensation issues for contingent workers
3. Key features of flexible work schedules, compressed workweeks, and telecommuting
4. Core and fringe compensation issues for flexible work schedules, compressed workweeks, and telecommuting
5. Unions' reactions to contingent workers and flexible work schedules
6. Strategic issues and choices in using contingent workers

Chapter Outline

I. **The Contingent Workforce**
 A. Groups of Contingent Workers
 B. Reasons for U.S. Employers' Increased Reliance on Contingent Workers

II. **Core and Fringe Compensation for Contingent Workers**
 A. Part-Time Employees
 B. Temporary Employees
 C. Leased Employees
 D. Independent Contractors, Freelancers, and Consultants

III. **Flexible Work Schedules: Flextime, Compressed Workweeks, and Telecommuting**
 A. Flextime Schedules
 B. Compressed Workweek Schedules
 C. Telecommuting
 D. Balancing the Demands of Work Life and Home Life

IV. **Core and Fringe Compensation for Flexible Employees**
 A. Core Compensation
 B. Fringe Compensation

V. **Unions' Reactions to Contingent Workers and Flexible Workers**
    A. Lowest-Cost Competitive Strategy
    B. Differentiation Competitive Strategy

Key Terms

Banking hours refer to a feature of flextime schedules that allows employees to vary the number of hours they work each day as long as they work a set number of hours each week. (p. 338)

Compressed workweek schedules enable employees to perform their full-time weekly work obligations in fewer days than a regular five-day workweek. (p. 338)

Consultants (independent contractors) are contingent workers who typically possess specialized skills that are in short supply in the labor market. Companies select independent contractors to complete particular projects of short-term duration—usually a year or less. (p. 329)

Contingent workers engage in explicitly tentative employment relationships with companies. (p. 324)

Core employees possess full-time jobs, and they generally plan long-term or indefinite relationships with their employers. (p. 324)

Core hours applies to flextime schedules, namely, the hours when all workers must be present. (p. 338)

Direct-hire arrangements refer to companies' recruitment and selection of temporary workers without assistance from employment agencies. (p. 328)

Dual-employer common law doctrine establishes temporary workers' rights to receive workers' compensation. (p. 334)

Economic reality test helps companies determine whether employees are financially dependent on them. (p. 336)

Flextime schedules allow employees to modify work schedules within specified limits set by the employer. (p. 336)

Freelancers (independent contractors) are contingent workers who typically possess specialized skills that are in short supply in the labor market. Companies select independent contractors to complete particular projects of short-term duration—usually a year or less. (p. 329)

Groupthink occurs when all group members agree on mistaken solutions because they share the same mind-set and view issues through the lens of conformity. (p. 343)

Independent contractors (freelancers) are contingent workers who typically possess specialized skills that are in short supply in the labor market. Companies select independent contractors to complete particular projects of short-term duration—usually a year or less. (p. 329)

Lease companies employ qualified individuals who they place in client companies on a long-term, presumably "permanent," basis. Lease companies place employees within client companies in exchange for fees. (p. 328)

On-call arrangements is a method for employing temporary workers. (p. 328)

Right-to-control test helps companies determine whether employed individuals are employees or independent contractors. (p. 335)

Telecommuting represents alternative work arrangements in which employees perform work at home or some other location besides the office. (p. 338)

Temporary employment agencies place individuals in client companies as employees on a temporary basis. (p. 327)

Voluntary part-time employees choose to work fewer than 35 hours per regularly scheduled workweek. (p. 325)

Working condition fringe benefits refer to the work equipment (for example, computer) and services (for example, an additional telephone line) employers purchase for telecommuters' use at home. (p. 341)

CHAPTER 14 REVIEW

Fill in the Blanks

Fill in the blanks with the appropriate terms.

A. Company loyalty
B. Voluntary
C. Contingent workers
D. Independent contractor
E. Temporary employees
F. Safe harbor rule
G. Groupthink
H. Direct-hire arrangements
I. Working condition fringe benefits
J. Job sharing
K. Dual-employer common law doctrine
L. Right-to-control test
M. Core employees
N. Economic reality test
O. Flexibility

1. Summer camp counselors are considered _____.

2. Another name for permanent, full-time workers is _____.

3. The _____ establishes temporary workers' rights to receive workers' compensation.

4. The _____ is used to determine whether employees are financially dependent on a company.

5. When an employer provides telecommuters with the necessary equipment to perform their jobs efficiently while off-site, it comes under the fringe compensation package known as _____.

6. _____ part-time employees choose to work fewer than 35 hours a week.

7. The key advantage of part-time workers for companies is _____.

8. Under _____, temporary employees typically do **not** work for more than one year.

9. An adjunct university faculty member represents a specific example of a/an _____.

10. Another name for part-time, temporary, or leased employees is _____.

11. Leasing companies are responsible for leased employees' retirement benefits when the _____ requirements are met.

12. _____ is when two or more part-time employees perform a single full-time job.

13. The IRS's _____ is used to determine whether employed individuals are employees or independent contractors.

14. _____ occurs when all team members agree on mistaken solutions because they share the same mind-set and view issues through the lens of conformity.

15. By relying more on contingent than full-time employees, companies generally trade cheaper labor costs and flexibility for _____.

Multiple-Choice Questions

Circle the correct answer for each question.

1. Under the *safe harbor rule*, leased employees **cannot** constitute more than what percent of the company's "non-highly compensated workforce"?

    A. 15%
    B. 20%
    C. 25%
    D. 30%

2. Which of the following is **not** a challenge mentioned when deciding on compensation for temporary employees?

    A. Will equity problems arise between the permanent employees and the temps?
    B. Must the temps be offered compensation benefits?
    C. Is the client company or the temp agency responsible for providing the benefits?
    D. How do the COBRA overtime provisions affect temporary employees?

3. Recently, companies have been hiring temporary employees for all **but** which of the following reasons?

    A. Temps offer employers the opportunity to evaluate whether a legitimate need exists to create a new full-time position.
    B. Good employees are hard to find.
    C. Temps give companies the opportunity to evaluate their performance for possible full-time employment.
    D. Temps are cheaper, as companies do not have to pay them benefits.

4. Part-time employees are eligible for retirement benefits if they are _____.

    A. 21 years old and have worked 1,000 hours
    B. 21 years old and have worked 15,000 hours
    C. 18 years old and have worked 1,000 hours
    D. 18 years old and have worked 1,500 hours

5. These temporary employees are generally placed with a company on a long-term, presumably permanent basis.

   A. Freelancers
   B. Leased
   C. Consultants
   D. Independent contractors

6. Client companies are responsible for providing leased employees group medical insurance, group life insurance, educational assistance programs, and continuation coverage requirements under

   A. COBRA.
   B. ERISA.
   C. FLSA.
   D. OSHA.

7. Which of the following was **not** given as a structural change that has lead to a rise in the use of contingent workers?

   A. Economic recessions
   B. More female workers in the workforce
   C. The shift from a service to a manufacturing economy
   D. International competition

8. Part-time employees who are given health insurance coverage under an employer-sponsored plan are entitled to protection under which federal law?

   A. Consolidated Omnibus Budget Reconciliation Act
   B. Fair Labor Standards Act
   C. National Employees Benefits Act
   D. Social Security Act

9. According to the mandates set down by this federal law, part-time workers must be paid according to federal overtime and minimum wage regulations.

   A. Employment Standards Act
   B. Title VII of the Civil Rights Act
   C. National Labor Relations Act
   D. Fair Labor Standards Act

10. Which of the following compensation challenges to companies who hire temporary employees was **not** cited in the readings?

    A. Should temps be part of a minority race?
    B. Should temps be given full benefits?
    C. Do equity problems arise between permanent full-time employees and temps?
    D. Should temps be paid hourly wages or salaries?

11. Temporary employees are eligible for qualified pension benefits if they meet the minimum service requirements set down by

    A. COBRA.
    B. ERISA.
    C. FLSA.
    D. OSHA.

12. The practice of requiring workers to be present during certain workday hours when business activity is regularly high is referred to as

    A. invariable hour.
    B. inflexible hours.
    C. core hours.
    D. banking hours.

13. The practice of varying the number of daily work hours, while maintaining the regular number of required weekly work hours, is referred to as

    A. variable hours.
    B. flex hours.
    C. core hours.
    D. banking hours.

14. This type of schedule enables employees to work four 10-hour days, three 12-hour days, or five 8-hour days in a given week.

    A. Banking hours workweek schedule
    B. Compressed workweek schedule
    C. Variable workweek schedule
    D. Flex schedule

15. Which of the following was **not** mentioned as a reason for increased short-term training costs for contingent workers?

    A. The longer time it takes a longer time to train the contingent employees
    B. The costs of the trainers and the materials
    C. Inefficiencies that may result until employees complete the training
    D. Downtime while employees train

Computer Exercise 14

Compensating Temporary Employees

Pizza Joe's Peoria, Illinois Plant Manager has decided that he has to hire more Pizza Makers to keep up with growing demand. Based on historic demand he's confident that he needs at least 4 more Pizza Makers, but he could use a total of 8 for at least the next 6 months. Pizza Joe's is looking for smart, hard working employees who can handle a variety of tasks. Turnover hurts productivity because all Pizza Makers must be trained in the plant. The position pays from $7.50 to 10.50 per hour depending on experience and skill level, and benefits average 38% of earnings. The average pay is $9.50 per hour. The plant manager estimates that training costs run about $1,000 in the first six months and that new employees are only about 50% as productive as trained workers during this period. After the first six months, those who successfully complete probation receive $8.50 per hour.

A temporary agency has offered to provide the plant with temporary Pizza Makers for $8.50 per hour. The employees would receive $6.00 per hour and no discretionary benefits. Pizza Joe's can hire any of the temps as regular employees without a fee after 6 months of temporary service. The agency will screen candidates per Pizza Joe's specifications, replace any workers that do not work out, pay all legally required benefits, and handle payroll. Pizza Joe's recruiter estimates that it will cost Pizza Joe between $1,000 to $2,000 per hire in staff time and recruitment expenses if Pizza Joe's does not use the agency.

Questions

Use the computer calculator to answer the questions below, enter your answers on the Answer Sheets, complete the exercise and print.

1. Compare the cost of employing 8 regular entry Pizza Makers for 6 months with the cost of using 8 temporary agency Pizza Makers for 6 months. Prepare 2 separate estimates for the regular hires. Base one on the lowest estimate of recruitment expenses and the other on the highest.

2. Calculate the cost of employing 4 regular entry Pizza Makers **and** 4 temporary agency Pizza Makers for 6 months. (Use the $2,000 per hire recruitment estimate.)

3. Assume that benefit costs for 8 entry Pizza Makers for 6 months equal $24,000. Determine the cost of 6 months of benefits for this group under the following situations.

A. Benefit costs rise by 5% per year for 3 years. What are the benefit costs at the end of years 1, 2, and 3 ($24,000 X 1.05 = year 1, year 1 X 1.05 = yr 2, etc.)
B. Benefit costs rise by 10% per year for 3 years. What are the benefit costs at the end of years 1, 2, and 3?

Further Study

F1. The above calculations assume that the regular and temporary employees are equally productive and stable. Determine which option below would be the least expensive over a 12 month period and list the expenses for both. Remember to include the $1,000 training cost for each new worker during his/her first six months of work.

Option 1: You use 8 temporary agency employees for 6 months. Half of them are "returned to the agency" or quit after the first 6 months of work. Four are hired as regular employees at $8.50 an hour. (You waive probation to maintain internal equity.) During the second 6 month period, you must hire eight more agency employees to fill the four vacancies since you need full productivity. (Remember new employees only produce half as much as trained employees.)

Option 2: You hire 8 regular employees from the start, recruitment costs equal $2,000 per hire, and all the employees successfully complete probation. Note that their wage is $8.50 per hour during the second six months and benefit costs equal 38% of earnings during the entire period.

ANSWER SHEET

CHAPTER 1

Fill-in the Blanks

1. N   6. A   11. M
2. K   7. E   12. I
3. G   8. J   13. O
4. B   9. L   14. D
5. H   10. C   15. F

Multiple Choice

1. C   6. D   11. C
2. D   7. C   12. D
3. A   8. D   13. B
4. A   9. B   14. D
5. C   10. A   15. C

CHAPTER 2

Fill-in the Blanks

1. G   6. H   11. L
2. D   7. C   12. O
3. K   8. J   13. I
4. E   9. N   14. F
5. A   10. B   15. M

Multiple Choice

1. D   6. B   11. B
2. B   7. C   12. A
3. D   8. B   13. D
4. C   9. B   14. C
5. D   10. A   15. B

CHAPTER 3

Fill-in the Blanks

1. E   6. H   11. C
2. L   7. A   12. D
3. J   8. F   13. B
4. G   9. K   14. I
5. O   10. M   15. N

Multiple Choice

1. A   6. C   11. B
2. A   7. B   12. B
3. C   8. D   13. D
4. C   9. D   14. A
5. D   10. C   15. D

CHAPTER 4

Fill-in the Blanks

1. L
2. A
3. E
4. B
5. N
6. O
7. K
8. M
9. G
10. F
11. J
12. D
13. C
14. I
15. H

Multiple Choice

1. A
2. A
3. A
4. C
5. B
6. D
7. B
8. B
9. A
10. B
11. D
12. A
13. D
14. C
15. C

CHAPTER 5

Fill-in the Blanks

1. C
2. A
3. O
4. F
5. H
6. E
7. G
8. I
9. L
10. J
11. D
12. B
13. J
14. N
15. M

Multiple Choice

1. B
2. D
3. B
4. C
5. A
6. A
7. D
8. C
9. D
10. C
11. C
12. A
13. D
14. D
15. A

CHAPTER 6

Fill-in the Blanks

1. L
2. B
3. F
4. C
5. O
6. K
7. M
8. A
9. D
10. E
11. G
12. J
13. N
14. I
15. H

Multiple Choice

1. B
2. B
3. C
4. A
5. A
6. C
7. B
8. A
9. D
10. D
11. C
12. C
13. D
14. B
15. B

CHAPTER 7

Fill-in the Blanks

1. M
2. C
3. O
4. E
5. G
6. B
7. A
8. D
9. F
10. J
11. L
12. K
13. H
14. N
15. I

Multiple Choice

1. D
2. C
3. A
4. C
5. A
6. D
7. C
8. C
9. A
10. D
11. D
12. B
13. C
14. A
15. B

CHAPTER 8

Fill-in the Blanks

1. N
2. J
3. B
4. E
5. F
6. C
7. O
8. D
9. G
10. L
11. I
12. K
13. M
14. H
15. A

Multiple Choice

1. B
2. D
3. C
4. A
5. C
6. D
7. A
8. B
9. D
10. B
11. D
12. A
13. A
14. B
15. C

CHAPTER 9

Fill-in the Blanks

1. F
2. B
3. L
4. A
5. G
6. I
7. D
8. M
9. C
10. J
11. K
12. H
13. N
14. E
15. O

Multiple Choice

1. D
2. A
3. B
4. D
5. C
6. B
7. B
8. D
9. C
10. D
11. A
12. C
13. A
14. C
15. B

CHAPTER 10

Fill-in the Blanks

1. F
2. E
3. A
4. O
5. C
6. N
7. H
8. K
9. G
10. J
11. I
12. L
13. D
14. B
15. M

Multiple Choice

1. B
2. C
3. A
4. D
5. B
6. C
7. A
8. D
9. C
10. D
11. C
12. A
13. C
14. A
15. B

CHAPTER 11

Fill-in the Blanks

1. F
2. A
3. L
4. G
5. E
6. D
7. H
8. M
9. J
10. O
11. B
12. C
13. I
14. K
15. N

Multiple Choice

1. B
2. C
3. B
4. C
5. D
6. B
7. B
8. C
9. B
10. C
11. C
12. A
13. D
14. D
15. A

CHAPTER 12

Fill-in the Blanks

1. C
2. N
3. M
4. A
5. O
6. G
7. L
8. E
9. H
10. J
11. K
12. D
13. B
14. I
15. F

Multiple Choice

1. C
2. C
3. A
4. C
5. B
6. D
7. B
8. A
9. C
10. D
11. B
12. B
13. D
14. A
15. A

CHAPTER 13

Fill-in the Blanks

1. B
2. E
3. D
4. N
5. C
6. M
7. H
8. O
9. A
10. G
11. F
12. I
13. J
14. L
15. K

Multiple Choice

1. A
2. A
3. D
4. D
5. A
6. B
7. B
8. B
9. C
10. D
11. B
12. A
13. C
14. C
15. C

CHAPTER 14

Fill-in the Blanks

1. E
2. M
3. K
4. N
5. I
6. B
7. O
8. H
9. D
10. C
11. F
12. J
13. L
14. G
15. A

Multiple Choice

1. B
2. D
3. B
4. A
5. B
6. A
7. C
8. A
9. D
10. A
11. B
12. C
13. D
14. B
15. A

PRENTICE HALL END USER LICENSE AGREEMENT

READ THIS LICENSE CAREFULLY BEFORE OPENING THIS PACKAGE. BY OPENING THIS PACKAGE, YOU ARE AGREEING TO THE TERMS AND CONDITIONS OF THIS LICENSE. IF YOU DO NOT AGREE, DO NOT OPEN THE PACKAGE. PROMPTLY RETURN THE UNOPENED PACKAGE AND ALL ACCOMPANYING ITEMS TO THE PLACE YOU OBTAINED THEM FOR A FULL REFUND OF ANY SUMS YOU HAVE PAID FOR THE SOFTWARE. *THESE TERMS APPLY TO ALL LICENSED SOFTWARE ON THE DISK EXCEPT THAT THE TERMS FOR USE OF ANY SHAREWARE OR FREEWARE ON THE DISKETTES ARE AS SET FORTH IN THE ELECTRONIC LICENSE LOCATED ON THE DISK:*

1. GRANT OF LICENSE and OWNERSHIP: The enclosed computer programs ("Software") are licensed, not sold, to you by Prentice-Hall, Inc. ("We" or the "Company") and in consideration of your payment of the license fee, which is part of the price you paid and your agreement to these terms. We reserve any rights not granted to you. You own only the disk(s) but we and/or our licensors own the Software itself. This license allows you to use and display your copy of the Software on a single computer (i.e., with a single CPU) at a single location for academic use only, so long as you comply with the terms of this Agreement. You may make one copy for back up, or transfer your copy to another CPU, provided that the Software is usable on only one computer.

2. RESTRICTIONS: You may not transfer or distribute the Software or documentation to anyone else. Except for backup, you may not copy the documentation or the Software. You may not network the Software or otherwise use it on more than one computer or computer terminal at the same time. You may not reverse engineer, disassemble, decompile, modify, adapt, translate, or create derivative works based on the Software or the Documentation. You may be held legally responsible for any copying or copyright infringement which is caused by your failure to abide by the terms of these restrictions.

3. TERMINATION: This license is effective until terminated. This license will terminate automatically without notice from the Company if you fail to comply with any provisions or limitations of this license. Upon termination, you shall destroy the Documentation and all copies of the Software. All provisions of this Agreement as to limitation and disclaimer of warranties, limitation of liability, remedies or damages, and our ownership rights shall survive termination.

4. LIMITED WARRANTY AND DISCLAIMER OF WARRANTY: Company warrants that for a period of 60 days from the date you purchase this SOFTWARE (or purchase or adopt the accompanying textbook), the Software, when properly installed and used in accordance with the Documentation, will operate in substantial conformity with the description of the Software set forth in the Documentation, and that for a period of 30 days the disk(s) on which the Software is delivered shall be free from defects in materials and workmanship under normal use. The Company does not warrant that the Software will meet your requirements or that the operation of the Software will be uninterrupted or error-free. Your only remedy and the Company's only obligation under these limited warranties is, at the Company's option, return of the disk for a refund of any amounts paid for it by you or replacement of the disk. THIS LIMITED WARRANTY IS THE ONLY WARRANTY PROVIDED BY THE COMPANY AND ITS LICENSORS, AND THE COMPANY AND ITS LICENSORS DISCLAIM ALL OTHER WARRANTIES, EXPRESS OR IMPLIED, INCLUDING WITHOUT LIMITATION, THE IMPLIED WARRANTIES OF MERCHANTABILITY AND FITNESS FOR A PARTICULAR PURPOSE. THE COMPANY DOES NOT WARRANT, GUARANTEE OR MAKE ANY REPRESENTATION REGARDING THE ACCURACY, RELIABILITY, CURRENTNESS, USE, OR RESULTS OF USE, OF THE SOFTWARE.

5. LIMITATION OF REMEDIES AND DAMAGES: IN NO EVENT, SHALL THE COMPANY OR ITS EMPLOYEES, AGENTS, LICENSORS, OR CONTRACTORS BE LIABLE FOR ANY INCIDENTAL, INDIRECT, SPECIAL, OR CONSEQUENTIAL DAMAGES ARISING OUT OF OR IN CONNECTION WITH THIS LICENSE OR THE SOFTWARE, INCLUDING FOR LOSS OF USE, LOSS OF DATA, LOSS OF INCOME OR PROFIT, OR OTHER LOSSES, SUSTAINED AS A RESULT OF INJURY TO ANY PERSON, OR LOSS OF OR DAMAGE TO PROPERTY, OR CLAIMS OF

THIRD PARTIES, EVEN IF THE COMPANY OR AN AUTHORIZED REPRESENTATIVE OF THE COMPANY HAS BEEN ADVISED OF THE POSSIBILITY OF SUCH DAMAGES. IN NO EVENT SHALL THE LIABILITY OF THE COMPANY FOR DAMAGES WITH RESPECT TO THE SOFTWARE EXCEED THE AMOUNTS ACTUALLY PAID BY YOU, IF ANY, FOR THE SOFTWARE OR THE ACCOMPANYING TEXTBOOK. BECAUSE SOME JURISDICTIONS DO NOT ALLOW THE LIMITATION OF LIABILITY IN CERTAIN CIRCUMSTANCES, THE ABOVE LIMITATIONS MAY NOT ALWAYS APPLY TO YOU.

6. GENERAL: THIS AGREEMENT SHALL BE CONSTRUED IN ACCORDANCE WITH THE LAWS OF THE UNITED STATES OF AMERICA AND THE STATE OF NEW YORK, APPLICABLE TO CONTRACTS MADE IN NEW YORK, AND SHALL BENEFIT THE COMPANY, ITS AFFILIATES AND ASSIGNEES. THIS AGREEMENT IS THE COMPLETE AND EXCLUSIVE STATEMENT OF THE AGREEMENT BETWEEN YOU AND THE COMPANY AND SUPERSEDES ALL PROPOSALS OR PRIOR AGREEMENTS, ORAL, OR WRITTEN, AND ANY OTHER COMMUNICATIONS BETWEEN YOU AND THE COMPANY OR ANY REPRESENTATIVE OF THE COMPANY RELATING TO THE SUBJECT MATTER OF THIS AGREEMENT. If you are a U.S. Government user, this Software is licensed with "restricted rights" as set forth in subparagraphs (a)-(d) of the Commercial Computer-Restricted Rights clause at FAR 52.227-19 or in subparagraphs (c)(1)(ii) of the Rights in Technical Data and Computer Software clause at DFARS 252.227-7013, and similar clauses, as applicable.

Should you have any questions concerning this agreement or if you wish to contact the Company for any reason, please contact in writing:
Director of New Media
Higher Education Division
Prentice-Hall, Inc.
1 Lake Street
Upper Saddle River, NJ 07458